Praise for
The Nurse Manager's Guide to Budgeting & Finance

"The Nurse Manager's Guide to Budgeting & Finance *is an indispensable resource for nurse leaders at every stage. It translates complex financial concepts into clear, actionable guidance that empowers nurse managers to lead with confidence. Grounded in real-world practice, this book strengthens financial literacy while keeping patient care and workforce sustainability at the center. It pushes beyond the limits of any practice setting and into other areas where financial literacy is key to nurses serving successfully. It belongs on the desk of every nurse manager responsible for stewarding resources and driving operational excellence."*

–Cole Edmonson, DNP, RN, FAAN
CEO, Nurses on Boards Coalition

"Many nurse leaders inherit responsibility for multimillion-dollar budgets long before they feel fully prepared to manage them. Dr. AnnMarie Papa closes that gap with a practical, experience-based guide that makes financial stewardship approachable, relevant, and actionable. She reminds us that budgeting is about controlling expenses but, more importantly, it is about making informed decisions that strengthen teams, support quality outcomes, and ensure the long-term sustainability of patient care. This is a resource I wish every emerging nurse leader had on their desk."

–Stacey-Ann Okoth, PhD, DNP, MBA, RN, NEA-BC, FACHE
Mountain Region Chief Nurse Executive
CommonSpirit Health

"Dr. AnnMarie Papa has advanced the seminal work of Dr. Al Rundio with a contemporary and comprehensive 4th edition that meets the realities of today's healthcare environment. Each chapter serves as a practical, goto guide, equipping nurse leaders with the essential knowledge and competencies required to navigate and influence healthcare finance. In an era where financial acumen is inseparable from effective leadership, this resource empowers nursing leaders—from frontline managers to chief nursing officers—to confidently engage in financial decisionmaking and drive organizational success."

–Helene M. Burns, DNP, RN, NEA-BC, FAONL, FAAN
Chief Nurse Executive, Emeritus
Helene Burns, Executive Coaching, LLC

"This exceptional reference is both thorough and concise. For nursing leaders who undervalue fiscal management, Papa successfully links informed budgeting directly to enhanced patient outcomes. She delivers a comprehensive, easy-to-follow breakdown of everything a nurse leader must know about the financial planning process."

–Mark Goldstein, MSN, RN, EMT-P I/C, FAEN
Department of Emergency Medicine
Denver Health

"Dr. Papa has done an exceptional job building upon the work of Dr. Rundio in bringing a fresh, practical perspective to the newest edition of The Nurse Manager's Guide to Budgeting & Finance. *This book makes complex healthcare finance concepts understandable through real-world examples and actionable insights. It is an invaluable resource, not only for nurse managers but also for anyone who wants to better understand budgeting, financial decision-making, and the challenges facing today's healthcare leaders."*

–Kit Bredimus, DNP, RN, CNML, NE-BC, CENP,
NEA-BC, FACHE, FAONL, FNAP
Chief Nursing Officer, Midland Health

"This book belongs on the shelf of every nurse manager—and every aspiring one. AnnMarie Papa delivers practical guidance on one of the most underdeveloped leadership skills when a nurse moves from a clinical role to one in leadership: financial management. From budgeting and revenue streams to managing unpredictability, this book equips nurse leaders with the essential skills needed to lead with greater confidence."

–Fred Neis, RN, FACHE, FAEN
Founder & Managing Partner
AdvisorRN, LLC

"Every nurse manager and nurse leader should keep The Nurse Manager's Guide to Budgeting & Finance *within arm's reach. Dr. Papa equips nurse leaders to understand the fiscal realities of care delivery, advocate for nurses and patients with data that matters, and claim their seat as strategic partners in care decisions. This isn't just career-building. It's how nursing practice gets advanced."*

–Daniel R. Tipton
CEO, Tipton Health Communications

"This remarkable 4th edition is a must-read for all new designated nurse leaders. 'The business case for nursing' is a key success factor for the future outcome of a novice nurse leader. The chief executive and the chief financial officer will respect your knowledge, and so will the clinical nursing staff. This previous comment took me over 35 years to learn."

–Victoria L Rich, PhD, RN, FAAN
Senior Vice President of Nursing, University of Pennsylvania Medical Center (retired)
Dean of Nursing, University of South Florida (retired)

"The skills that make a nurse an excellent clinician are not the same skills required to succeed as a nurse leader. Managers and directors must be proficient in the language and mechanics of budgeting and finance, especially at this juncture in healthcare, with decreased reimbursement and shrinking resources. Knowing how to communicate staffing needs, budget variances, and revenue opportunities in financial terms to hospital administration is paramount. The Nurse Manager's Guide to Budgeting & Finance, *4th Edition, is a comprehensive and comprehendible review that provides the knowledge and tools for both the new and seasoned nursing leader. To paraphrase Sir Francis Bacon, 'Knowledge is power.' Given the knowledge and tools provided in this guide, a nurse can successfully transition from clinician to manager."*

–James Hoelz, MS, MBA, RN, CEN, FAEN
President/Founder, Blue Jay Consulting

the NURSE MANAGER'S GUIDE to BUDGETING & FINANCE

FOURTH EDITION

AnnMarie Papa, DNP, RN, CEN, NE-BC, FAEN, FAAN

Sigma
GLOBAL NURSING EXCELLENCE

Sigma Theta Tau International Honor Society of Nursing (Sigma) is a nonprofit organization whose mission is developing nurse leaders anywhere to improve healthcare everywhere. Founded in 1922, Sigma has more than 85,000 active members in over 100 countries and territories. Members include practicing nurses, instructors, researchers, policymakers, entrepreneurs, and others. Sigma's more than 630 chapters are located at more than 700 institutions of higher education throughout Armenia, Australia, Botswana, Brazil, Canada, Chile, Colombia, Croatia, England, Eswatini, Finland, Ghana, Hong Kong, Ireland, Israel, Italy, Jamaica, Japan, Jordan, Kenya, Lebanon, Malawi, Mexico, the Netherlands, Nigeria, Pakistan, Philippines, Portugal, Puerto Rico, Saudi Arabia, Scotland, Singapore, South Africa, South Korea, Spain, Sweden, Taiwan, Tanzania, Thailand, the United States, and Wales. Learn more at www.sigmanursing.org.

Sigma Theta Tau International
550 West North Street
Indianapolis, IN, USA 46202

To request a review copy for course adoption, order additional books, buy in bulk, or purchase for corporate use, contact Sigma Marketplace at 888.654.4968 (US/Canada toll-free), +1.317.687.2256 (International), or solutions@sigmamarketplace.org.

To request author information, or for speaker or other media requests, contact Sigma Marketing at 888.634.7575
(US/Canada toll-free) or +1.317.634.8171 (International).

ISBN:	9781646482221
EPUB ISBN:	9781646482238
PDF ISBN:	9781646482245

Library of Congress Control Number: 2026025204

Publisher: Dustin Sullivan
Acquisitions Editor: Emily Hatch
Development Editor: Jillmarie Leeper Sycamore
Cover Designer: Rebecca Batchelor
Interior Design/Page Layout: Rebecca Batchelor
Indexer: Cheryl Lenser

Managing Editor: Carla Hall
Technical Peer Reviewer: Brienne Sandow
Project Editor: Todd Lothery
Copy Editor: Todd Lothery
Proofreader: Erin Geile

This book is dedicated to the memory and legacy of our friend and colleague, Dr. Al Rundio. Reviewing and editing his masterpiece was a labor of love. Al was an amazing leader whose work inspired many. His work in this space has significantly impacted our profession. Budgeting is not a skill we learn in nursing school. It is one that we acquire after countless hours of practice and study. It is often said that if you know the budget in one hospital, you know it in one hospital, as each organization has a different approach. Al broke the glass ceiling with his first edition of this book, and I am honored to continue his legacy with this updated edition.

Acknowledgments

First I would like to acknowledge every CNO, COO, and CFO that had the patience to mentor me as a nursing leader. Some include Marion Tuck, PhD, RN; Beth Duffy; Joan Randolph, RN; Diane Corrigan; Tom Bilecky; and Gerry Blaney. Their partnership, guidance, support, and encouragement inspired me to learn more and work smarter.

And as we know, many things take a village. I would like to thank my colleagues: Beth Duffy, Senior Vice President, Jefferson Health; Dennis Pfleiger, President of St. Lukes Quakertown; Daniel Hudson, MSN, RN, CENP, SVP of Nursing Operations and CNO of Ambulatory Nursing at Jefferson Health; Dr. Andrew Thum, DNP, MP, RN, NEA-BC, Director of Nursing Workforce Operations, Jefferson Health; Dr. Nancy Mannion, DNP, RN, CEN, FAEN, FAAN, President of NMB Global; and Dr. Nicholas Chmielewski, DNP, RN, CEN, CENP, NEA-BC, FAEN, Associate Director, BRG. Their knowledge and expertise helped to fill the gaps and brought new perspectives to this work.

Finally, I would like to thank each of you for making an investment in your future as you use this book as a resource to expand your horizons, build your confidence, and lead the future of nursing.

About the Author

AnnMarie Papa, DNP, RN, CEN, NE-BC, FAEN, FAAN, is an energetic and engaging leader who mentors and inspires many. She has presented on many topics related to leadership and nursing regionally, nationally, and internationally. Holding a BSN and MSN from Villanova University and a DNP from Waynesburg University, Papa is also a Fellow in both the Academy of Emergency Nursing and the American Academy of Nursing.

With over 49 years of experience, Papa has a proven track record of successful team building, innovative problem-solving, and leadership development. She is an authentic, transformational, and servant leader with a strong background in organizational development. She consistently leads teams to enhance quality outcomes and fosters interprofessional collaboration and healthy work environments.

Papa is a thought leader and sought-after speaker on leadership, mentoring, and many other topics. She is a recipient of the National ENA Lifetime Achievement Award, Judith Kelleher Award, 2011 Villanova University College of Nursing Alumni Medallion, Health Leaders Media Top 20, and many other local, state, and national awards for leadership, professionalism, and team building. During the COVID-19 pandemic, she was recognized as a Legend in Nursing by Mainline Healthcare Leaders and received the DAISY Lifetime Achievement Award. In 2011 she served as the National ENA President and recently retired from her role of Vice President and Chief Nursing Officer at Jefferson Einstein Montgomery. Currently, Papa continues to serve the Jefferson Nursing Department as the inaugural Nurse Leader Emeritus.

Contributing Author

Nicholas Chmielewski (Chapter 12), DNP, RN, CEN, CENP, NEA-BC, FAEN, is a nationally recognized leader in emergency department operations and performance improvement. He leads an international consulting firm's Emergency Care Solutions team, bringing his more than 20 years of experience driving operational and financial transformation across more than 75 emergency departments in 21 states.

Chmielewski's expertise spans care delivery operations, budgeting, and data-driven decision-making, with a focus on aligning staffing models, patient flow, and financial performance to achieve sustainable outcomes. He has served in executive nursing leadership roles, including Health System Director and Associate Chief Nursing Officer positions, and is recognized for translating complex operational data into practical strategies for multidisciplinary teams.

A published author and national speaker, Chmielewski is known for translating evidence-based strategy into practical solutions for emergency department leaders. His thought leadership helps organizations improve performance, strengthen workforce models, and sustain high-quality care amid growing operational complexity.

Special Note to Readers

Here at Sigma, we realize that language is constantly evolving. The meaning of a word often changes over time, some words become obsolete, and some terms that were once acceptable may become controversial or even offensive, depending on the context or circumstances. We have made every effort to make language choices that are inclusive and not offensive. Should you identify words in this book that you believe negatively impact a group or groups of people, please reach out to us at Publications@SigmaNursing.org.

Table of Contents

Foreword

I vividly recall my introduction to nursing finance. At the time, I was a trauma clinical nurse specialist (CNS) who was unexpectedly asked to assume the trauma coordinator role after my predecessor accepted a new position. My educational background and professional experience had been firmly rooted in clinical practice—trauma, critical care, and emergency nursing. The highest-level leadership role I had held was that of ED charge nurse. Suddenly, I found myself responsible not only for managing a small team of trauma program staff but also for overseeing the program's budget.

When the nursing director reviewed my new responsibilities, she handed me a spreadsheet dense with numbers and unfamiliar financial terms. She spoke of operating and capital budgets, variances, and the organization's expectation that I manage our budget within approved parameters. Like any leader in the health system, I was expected to seek approval for and fully justify any expenses that fell outside the established budget, as well as prepare and defend our operating and capital budget requests for the next fiscal year. I was also given the authority to review expenditures and approve or deny them according to our budget guidelines. For someone who had never imagined moving into a formal nursing leadership role, I felt wholly unprepared.

I was a stranger in a strange land. Despite my initial "deer in the headlights" reaction to all things budget—which I hoped I concealed better than I probably did—I recognized one certainty early in my new role—to advocate effectively for my program, my team, and ultimately our patients, I had to learn, understand, and become *fluent* in the language of budgeting and finance. It quickly became clear that the finance personnel I met were not about to learn the clinical language of healthcare. I had to serve as the bridge, translating our needs into terms they could understand.

My first step was to enroll in a post-graduate certificate program in nursing administration at the same university where I had earned my master's degree in the CNS track. One of the early curriculum requirements was a nursing finance course taught by a former hospital financial officer. Bingo. That was precisely where I needed to begin—and it felt like a lifeline. The course introduced key financial terms and standard methods for reporting financial performance. That class, together with subsequent coursework in the post-master's nursing administration certificate program, provided a foundation I would draw on as I advanced through progressively higher levels of nursing leadership, from coordinator to program manager, director, and eventually system-level vice president.

Becoming financially savvy is an expectation of nurse leaders and strengthens their ability to exert influence. Although the language and concepts may seem foreign at first, developing competence in this domain enables nurse leaders to advocate more effectively for the resources they need and to earn a seat at the decision-making table. Nurse leaders must think critically and evaluate proposals and actions across multiple domains, including their potential financial risks and benefits. Because no institution has an unlimited budget, the ability to make fiscally sound decisions is essential. Equally important is the ability to build a compelling case, grounded in sound financial justification, to secure necessary resources. Together, these competencies position nurse leaders for success and help them prioritize healthcare spending wisely.

When I think back on my introduction to the financial world of healthcare, I realize I initially learned individual budget terms and financial concepts without fully understanding the larger healthcare ecosystem. That broader perspective came only with years of experience and more advanced finance courses.

What impresses me most about AnnMarie Papa's revision of Al Rundio's classic work, *The Nurse Manager's Guide to Budgeting & Finance*, is the way it equips nurse leaders with essential knowledge in a practical, real-world context. It is not merely a compilation of financial terms and formulas, as so many finance books are, but an integrated guide that helps nurse leaders see the broader picture, allowing the finer details of budgeting to fall into place within a meaningful framework. It also offers important background on the external laws, regulations, and financial pressures that healthcare organizations must navigate to secure reimbursement for services.

In this fourth edition, AnnMarie Papa has done a remarkable job updating Al Rundio's text to reflect today's financial challenges and opportunities, helping nurse leaders function more competently and confidently in their roles. She brings to this work the depth of experience that comes from advancing through progressive nursing management positions and serving as a chief nursing officer in a major health system. She has edited this edition with a clear understanding of what nurses and nurse leaders need most. I have known AnnMarie for many years. She is a nurse's nurse, and this book will serve as a trusted guide for readers as they navigate their own leadership journey into the world of finance.

In closing, much as we as nurses would like to care for patients altruistically, without concern for the finances that support the delivery system, such a model is not sustainable unless the necessary resources are in place. It is the nurse leader's responsibility to advocate for and steward those resources so that nurses, support staff, and other clinicians can focus their efforts where they belong: on the patient. Keep this book close at hand. It will be an invaluable companion as you find your footing and equip you to lead with greater clarity, confidence, and credibility in the financial arena of healthcare.

–Linda Laskowski-Jones, MS, APRN, ACNS-BC, CEN, NEA-BC,
FAWM, FAEN, FAAN
Editor-in-Chief, *Nursing*
Health, Learning, Research, and Practice, Wolters Kluwer

> "Everything that can be counted does not necessarily count; everything that counts cannot necessarily be counted."
>
> –Albert Einstein, theoretical physicist, 1879–1955

Introduction

Welcome to the fourth edition of *The Nurse Manager's Guide to Budgeting & Finance*. Dr. Al Rundio first published this book in 2012 as a resource and guide to help nurse managers navigate the challenging world of finance. This new edition continues to build on that vision.

NOTE

Throughout the book, some of Al Rundio's examples remain, and are indicated as such. Any other material is that of the current author, AnnMarie Papa.

Each chapter tackles a different tenet of finance, budgets, and the budgeting process. The chapters are interdependent and can be used individually or as a whole.

Many nurses become nurse managers as the next necessary step to advance in their careers. Some form a desire to contribute to nurses and nursing within their organization. Often, though, nurses find themselves in a management position without the tools and skills needed to do the job effectively.

As revenues decrease in most healthcare facilities, more pressure is placed on nurse managers to manage the organization's resources—both human capital and supplies—more judiciously. Suddenly, they need to understand words and phrases like *productivity, variance* and *staffing to census*. To manage the organization's resources more wisely, nurse managers must be armed with the necessary tools and information to do the job well. After all, healthcare is a business.

Nurse managers must possess some basic knowledge about budgeting and finance. The reality is that each nurse manager is managing their own business (the nursing unit) within the organization. With decreasing revenue streams, nurse managers must manage their units so that actual expenses equal budgeted expenses, or they must be able to justify variances and take corrective action where needed. Nurse managers must also be familiar with certain types of budget reports, how to interpret these reports, and, most importantly, how to take action to control the results.

This book is written for the nurse manager at the unit level and above in any healthcare organization. It's a handbook that is intended to be used on the job for the effective management of the organization's finances. It is also intended to share with nurse managers concepts that can be implemented in management so they become more effective at managing the resources of the organization. Finally, this book will assist any nursing manager pursuing certification as a nurse executive.

Healthcare in the United States—where this book's primary audience practices—is different from that of many other countries, especially those with a national single-payer health plan. The US has numerous insurance products on the market. US citizens generally receive health benefits from their employers, which are subsidized by the employee. Some individuals purchase an entire insurance product on their own. The elderly and certain patient populations—such as dialysis patients—receive Medicare. The poor can receive Medicaid. The Children's Health Insurance Program covers otherwise uninsured children. Medicare and Medicaid are the two federal programs for healthcare insurance. The Patient Protection and Affordable Care Act (ACA) of 2010 has assisted millions more individuals with health insurance through the health insurance marketplace.

In the US, healthcare costs continue to rise. Insured Americans are experiencing tighter controls from insurance plans, where second and third opinions for certain elective procedures may be required and where certain medications need approval from the insurance company.

NOTE

Although the US system does have financial problems, it's not the only one. National single-payer systems also have financial problems—sometimes equal to or greater than those in the US. A free-market system, like the one in the US, creates competition, which can lower rates as well as add services and products.

An estimated 25.3 million Americans ages 0-64 have no health insurance at all as of 2023, as reported by the Kaiser Family Foundation (Tolbert et al., 2026). The National Center for Health Statistics reports 27.2 million uninsured in 2024, including all ages (Centers for Disease Control and Prevention, 2025). The ACA has helped address this problem by making insurance exchanges available and assessing financial penalties if an uninsured person does not purchase health insurance. (Since its passage, there have been many challenges to this act. The federal government no longer assesses financial penalties for uninsured persons. Some state governments do, however.) Those without health insurance might not seek healthcare when needed and might not seek primary care for the prevention of illness. This is obviously a problem. However, another problem is created as more Americans obtain health insurance: There are not enough primary care providers to serve them all. Thus, long delays to access health services may result.

This reality places advanced practice nurses in a pivotal position to become the primary care providers of the nation—a notion promoted by the American Academy of Medicine, whose 2021 report *The Future of Nursing 2020–2030* calls for all nurses to function at their full scope of practice.

The uniqueness of healthcare reimbursement in the US and the fact that the US is the top-most industrialized country in the world that does not provide universal healthcare to all citizens means nurse managers must balance cost with quality. To effectively do this, nurse managers must understand the basic concepts of budgeting. These concepts are the essence of this book for the nurse manager.

The fourth edition of *The Nurse Manager's Guide to Budgeting & Finance* takes a deeper dive into the nursing budget than the previous editions. New information includes reimbursement in other practice settings such as primary care offices, urgent care centers, same-day surgery centers, and long-term facilities, including nursing homes and assisted living facilities. This new edition also expands coverage of the Quality and Safety Education for Nurses (QSEN) competencies for graduate nursing education and their relationship to budgeting and finance. It adds more information on boards, including the difference between a system network board and a hospital board.

Chapters in this book cover the following key information:

- **Chapter 1, "Budgeting for the Nurse Manager":** This chapter covers the budgeting process for nurse managers and its relationship to patient care. It contains information on not-for-profit and for-profit hospitals and other healthcare systems and care settings. It discusses what a budget is, the benefits of budgeting, and the integral nature of budgeting. Finally, it includes an interview with a nurse manager of an emergency department.
- **Chapter 2, "Healthcare Reimbursement":** This chapter covers a significant amount of material on the political history of healthcare and an overview of healthcare reimbursement in the US, including

reimbursement for long-term care. It discusses the role of policy in healthcare reimbursement and the importance of reimbursement. Finally, it touches on the effect of the COVID-19 pandemic on healthcare.

- **Chapter 3, "Budget Types":** This chapter discusses assets, liability, and equity and defines several other basic accounting terms. Responsibility center budgeting is also discussed, followed by forms of budgets, historical budgets, operating budgets, and capital budgets. Finally, it covers the importance of strategic vision and mission and the cash basis of accounting.
- **Chapter 4, "Budget Development":** This chapter covers the steps of the budget-development workflow, including collecting data, planning services, planning activities, implementing the plan, monitoring the budget, and taking corrective action when necessary. It also discusses management's role in budgeting and inventory management. Finally, it includes an interview with a chief nursing officer, with a focus on how the COVID-19 pandemic has affected nursing.
- **Chapter 5, "Operating Budgets":** This chapter takes a deeper dive into key concepts in the development of an operating budget. It covers key metrics, discusses expenses, and illustrates how to calculate employee-related costs. It discusses outpatient reimbursement and debunks various budgeting myths.
- **Chapter 6, "Capital Budgets":** This chapter covers budgeting for major movable equipment and for fixed assets. It provides examples of capital expenses. It explains why you need to develop a capital budget and how to do it. Finally, it discusses the importance of including a contingency line in capital budgets.
- **Chapter 7, "Budget Variances":** In this chapter, readers learn how to conduct variance analysis, calculate variances, assess efficiency and cost variances, and avoid negative cost variances.

- **Chapter 8, "Budget Reports":** In this chapter, you'll find a discussion of types of budget reports and several examples of staff reports, including a new report on nursing salary variances.
- **Chapter 9, "Healthcare Reform and the Affordable Care Act":** This chapter discusses the need for healthcare reform and includes updated information on the ACA of 2010 (including major challenges to this act). Hospital mergers, closures, strategic partnering, and global caps are also discussed.
- **Chapter 10, "Governing Boards of Healthcare Organizations and Specialty Nursing Organizations":** This chapter explains what governing boards are (including the differences between a health system network board and a hospital board) and identifies their responsibilities. It defines conflicts of interest, cites common mistakes made by governing boards, and discusses the role of nurses on governing boards. It then shifts to a discussion of specialty organizations: what they are, how their governing boards work, and how they develop budgets.
- **Chapter 11, "Improving Quality and Safety to Increase Reimbursement":** This chapter has been expanded to cover the QSEN program, incentivizing quality (for example, by using value-based incentives), the role of nursing in improving quality, quality and population health, assessing home-care quality, and high-reliability organizations.
- **Chapter 12, "Artificial Intelligence Budgeting Considerations":** The term *artificial intelligence* (AI) commonly refers to the application of machine learning techniques to large datasets (predictive modeling) and the emergence of computer systems generating content (generative tools). At the time of this publication, AI's use is rapidly expanding in healthcare, both in aiding/supporting clinical practice and in administrative supporting functions. This chapter discusses AI policy, budget, and use considerations for the nurse manager.

- **Chapter 13, "Conclusions":** This chapter discusses the importance of getting politically involved, knowing what types of insurance plans reimburse your organization, developing strategic relationships with key individuals in your organization, speaking the language of finance, practicing finance, and embracing change.

Case examples and interviews have been added to a number of the chapters to further demonstrate the concepts being presented. These should assist you in mastering the principles of budgeting and finance.

If you're ready to improve your ability to successfully manage a nursing unit or department or to simply gain a better understanding of budgeting and finance in healthcare, read on!

It is my hope that this book will be a valuable resource for you throughout your career. It has always been said that "knowledge is power." There is a wealth of knowledge to be garnered in this new edition. Take it, embrace it, synthesize it, and utilize it to make a difference. I wish each of you great success for the future as we work to navigate the complex, challenging, and exciting world of nursing!

References

Centers for Disease Control and Prevention. (2025, June 24). *U.S. uninsured rate drops by 15% since 2020*. National Center for Health Statistics. https://www.cdc.gov/nchs/pressroom/releases/20250624.html

National Academies of Sciences, Engineering, and Medicine. (2021). *The future of nursing 2020–2030*. National Academies Press.

Tolbert, J., Cervantes, S., Bell, C., & Damico, A. (2026, April 9). *Key facts about the uninsured population*. Kaiser Family Foundation. https://www.kff.org/uninsured/key-facts-about-the-uninsured-population/

Budgeting for the Nurse Manager

Al's first nurse manager job was at an urban emergency department (ED) where the director of nursing generated and monitored the budget, and managers did not have a clue about managing the budget. My first job was at a small community ED, and I reported directly to the chief nursing officer. While I was expected to have some basic budgeting knowledge, I was given guidance and education to help me hone those skills. I took a budgeting class at New York University and spent hours in the library working to understand variances, hours per patient day/visit, productive and nonproductive time, financial lingo, and many other budgeting skills, which will be explained in detail throughout this book.

As nurse manager, it is important to understand what information you need so that you can successfully manage and own your budgets. Unfortunately, this is an area for which many do not receive guidance or may be reluctant to ask!

The Budgeting Process for Nurse Managers and Its Relationship to Patient Care

Of course, many nurses are happy to avoid the nitty-gritty accounting details inherent in the development and management of a budget. This head-in-the-sand attitude with regard to financial affairs is perhaps understandable. After all, we went into nursing to care for patients. But what many of us often fail to remember is that caring for patients requires prioritizing needs and allocating finite resources. This requires budgeting.

Budgeting and finance are not addressed adequately in the typical nursing curriculum. This is understandable because nurses need to learn many things about clinical care, and so the curriculum focuses on that. Nurses get more exposure to finance and budgeting at the master's degree level, and those who pursue a nursing management degree learn the most about these topics.

A lot of nurses think that it is up to the nurse manager on the unit to worry about and manage the budget. However, the reality is that every item that we use has a cost associated with it that affects the budget—and thus the dollars—of the organization. You'd have to be living in a vacuum to miss how the general economy affects your own life; the same is true in healthcare. There is not a bottomless pit of money and reimbursement.

Every nurse and other hospital employee must be accountable for the use of resources. Nurses who understand the budgeting process will be able to contribute positively to organizational performance and ensure organizational sustainability. Sharing the budget with the frontline staff helps them understand the impact of their work. Often they are the best source of ideas for how best to reduce costs as well.

Besides, although understanding financial and budgeting concepts can be challenging, it can also be exciting, and everyone should become well versed on these topics. After all, nursing is many professions rolled into one—and fiscal management should not be excluded.

NOTE

In today's healthcare environment, managers are held accountable for the financial performance of their units. As President Harry Truman stated so well, "The buck stops here." At the same time, managers must have the authority and resources to carry out the functions for that unit.

Nonprofit Versus For-Profit Healthcare Organizations

Before beginning your budgeting journey, it's important for you to understand the distinctions between the two major types of healthcare organizations: nonprofit organizations and for-profit organizations.

A majority of nurses today are employed in nonprofit hospitals or health systems. The American Hospital Association (2026) reports that nonprofit hospitals make up 58% of the US's 5,121 community hospitals. The history of healthcare sheds light on why. Originally, hospitals were charity organizations that provided care to dying patients. Care was free. Because hospitals provided care to the communities they served, hospitals initially were nonprofit to maintain tax-exempt status. However, since the 1990s, an increase in for-profit hospitals and health systems has occurred.

You're probably wondering: How do nonprofit healthcare organizations differ from for-profit ones? The major differences are as follows (Hart, 2023):

- A nonprofit hospital does not pay state or local property taxes or federal income taxes. The organization is considered to be a charity and provides certain community benefits in accordance with local needs and state and federal Internal Revenue Service (IRS) guidelines.
- A for-profit hospital or health system is owned either by private investors or public shareholders. The organization is part of a company

that issues shares of stock to raise revenue to expand the hospital or health system's activities.

Historically, for-profit hospitals were mostly based in the southern part of the United States—generally in Florida and Texas. For example, HCA Healthcare is a large for-profit health system that began in Tennessee and was concentrated in Florida and Texas, primarily. However, in recent decades, investor-owned hospitals have expanded nationally. For example, beginning in the 1980s, HCA Healthcare began acquiring other healthcare corporations and expanding its coverage (HCA Healthcare, 2026) and now operates in 19 states and the UK (Cass, 2025). Often, these hospital systems have purchased financially distressed facilities or stand-alone hospitals that need access to capital to expand. Depending on prevailing economic conditions, for-profit hospitals can gain better access to capital than nonprofit hospitals that expand by issuing debt through tax-exempt bonds.

Under Centers for Medicare & Medicaid Services standards, a nonprofit hospital is generally defined as a hospital that is organized as a nonprofit entity and operates under the Internal Revenue Code Section 501(c)(3) charitable organization classification. This means it is exempt from federal income tax and must meet specific IRS requirements for charitable status (Congress.gov, 2024). As we have seen recently, many smaller stand-alone hospitals have merged with larger systems, some hospitals have closed their doors totally, and newer, more complex systems are now prevalent. This places even more challenges on the individual nurse manager. Understanding the data is essential to the fiscal success of each unit and the entire organization.

The reality is that as cost containment becomes more critical and resources more restrained, many stand-alone hospitals will need to merge with larger systems, some of which will most certainly be for-profit health systems. Understanding the nuances of finance and budgeting enables you to keep the patient at the center and communicate your needs to the teams in factual and knowledgeable terms.

Other Care Settings

In addition to hospitals, nurse managers practice in a variety of other care settings, including:

- Long-term care facilities, including nursing homes and assisted-living facilities
- Primary care offices
- Urgent care centers
- Same-day surgery centers
- Rehabilitation centers, such as physical rehabilitation centers and residential centers for the treatment of addiction
- Home care agencies

As is the case with hospitals, some of these are for-profit organizations, while others are nonprofit organizations. In addition, some of these organizations are part of a larger hospital system—for example, primary care offices and urgent care centers. Others stand alone.

Generally, the same principles on budgeting apply to these organizations. Dollar amounts, however, will be different. For example, instead of nursing hours per patient day, staffing usually will be defined by the number of patient visits or procedures. The focus on quality patient care—which is vital for maximizing reimbursement—will also be the same.

What Is a Budget?

Before you can explore the finer points of budgeting, it's critical to answer this question: What is a budget? A *budget* is all of the following (Jones et al., 2018):

- A forecast of the resources required to deliver the services offered by an organization

"A budget is more than just numbers on a page. It is the embodiment of our values."

–Barack Obama

- A plan for coordinating the financial goals of an organization
- A blueprint
- A formal, quantitative expression of management's plans, intentions, expectations, and actions to control results

The primary purpose of a budget is to manage and control costs. A budget is based on an organization's mission, values, and strategic plan. If the budget is forecasted properly—which involves comprehensive data assessment—the actual outcomes will come close to the predicted outcomes.

NOTE

A key aspect of the nurse manager's job is to achieve the goals and objectives of the organization. Today, that involves meeting those goals and objectives in a cost-effective manner.

The budgeting process has three primary objectives:

- To establish an annual and a monthly budget
- To identify and analyze actual experience compared to the budget plan
- To accurately report all financial and statistical data

Budgeting involves converting an operating plan into financial terms by outlining resources to achieve the organization's goals and objectives. It is a managerial process driven by strategy, goals and objectives, and industry trends. Ultimately, a budget provides an organization with a financial road map.

NOTE

Budgeting is meant to prep an organization for the future, to communicate expectations regarding the organization's operating functions, and to allocate resources among competing demands within the organization.

The Benefits of Budgeting

"A budget tells your money where to go, instead of wondering where it went."

–Dave Ramsey

The budgeting process is essential to a well-functioning organization. Generally, the budget provides a forecast of what will occur during a one-year time frame. It is a quantitative expression of management's plans, intentions, and actions. It quantifies the strategic goals of the organization.

While the budgeting process is not optional, the degree and formality of unit-level ownership vary. Investing time in a well-planned budget will yield a future return on investment: the sustainment of the organization's viability. After they are created, budgets are communicated to all key partners so that everyone is on the same page.

Although managers are held accountable for the budgeting process, as well as for monitoring operations to ensure compliance with the budget, all staff must contribute to budget performance through the judicious use of supplies and labor.

NOTE

Nurse managers must make every effort to turn a positive bottom line. Nurse managers who contribute positively to the organization's bottom line will impact the success and continued operation of the organization.

Benefits of budgeting include:

- **Budgeting places everyone on the management team.** The one thing that every department manager in an organization must develop and use is the budget. Each departmental budget contributes to the overall organizational budget. All managers are held accountable for their budget performance.
- **Budgeting helps create cost awareness.** Budgeting is the formal, quantitative expression of management's plans and attention. Paying attention to numbers fosters greater cost awareness within the organization.
- **Budgeting can produce cost savings.** Budgets often require managers to justify every cost, expense, and revenue and can help them identify more cost-effective alternatives (such as zero-based budgeting). Simply put, budgets produce cost savings because the budgeting process creates cost awareness.
- **Budgeting can reduce waste.** As cost awareness increases, nurse managers can focus on what costs can be reduced or eliminated, thus reducing waste in the organization.
- **Budgeting helps measure individual and departmental productivity and profitability.** All nurse managers must think of their responsibility center as their own business. They must recognize that they manage a business and strive to ensure that the business survives. In other words, the business must be profitable. The ultimate goal is to generate a positive operating margin so that hospitals are able to continue serving our patients and communities. Many hospitals and healthcare facilities have closed in our nation because of poor business and management practices.
- **Budgeting minimizes operational surprises.** These surprises include cash shortages, operating losses, and so on. Budgets eliminate operational surprises because they create a plan for expenses. A CEO Al worked with never assessed the needs of surgeons regarding capital

equipment (major movable equipment) requests. His feeling was that surgeons always wanted expensive devices, so it was best not to ask. Al felt the opposite. At budget-preparation time, he sent a memo to each surgical department chief to ask what their capital budget needs were for the following year. That way, he knew what to budget for. This significantly minimized operational surprises, such as a surgeon, mid-year, suddenly requesting a $100,000 piece of equipment that was not in the budget. My practice was to hang a list in the department and ask for input. Once the list was generated, I asked for their priority and often met with all staff to understand their thoughts as well as explain the organizational imperatives.

- **Budgeting provides all levels of management with a set of predetermined operating standards with which to evaluate performance.** Budgeting places all managers on the same page, so to speak. Even though each department has different budget requirements, certain items remain standard across all departments—for example, across-the-board raises for employees and the percentage costs of employee benefits.
- **Budgeting communicates organizational goals and objectives.** The budget ties directly to organizational goals and objectives; indeed, it's what enables these goals and objectives to be achieved. By going through the budgeting process, managers become aware of these organizational goals and objectives.
- **Budgeting serves as an excellent means of educating and developing nurse managers.** An organization's finance department can offer nurse managers an excellent education in budgeting, fiscal management, and fiscal accountability. Al explained that when he served as a chief nursing officer at one hospital, his finance department taught him a great deal about fiscal management. He learned terms such as *in the aggregate* (the big picture), *amortization* (when payment for a costly purchase is spread out over time), and so on. They provided him with an education that made him unafraid of budgets and finance. In my own experience as nursing director of the ED at a busy

urban hospital, we met with the chief financial officer monthly. She was definitely a numbers person and had a direct and no-nonsense approach. As nursing directors we were expected to explain variances and predict changes. She challenged us to stretch and grow. She also did not always understand the nuances of each unit and appreciated us partnering with her to ensure both the patient and the organization received our best. She taught us to stand firm in our beliefs and how to speak in terms that enabled us to translate our beliefs and needs into workable information to best formulate the budget.

- **Budgeting frees top management to concentrate on developing strategies for future institutional growth.** It is up to all levels of management to manage the budget. However, it is really the frontline manager or the nurse manager at the unit level who needs to do the most with budgeting (and, let's face it, everything else). If frontline nurse managers develop—in collaboration with finance—a well-thought-out budget, implement and monitor it well, and take corrective action when necessary, the facility will run like a smooth-sailing ship. This frees up top executives in the organization to concentrate on what they need to do—for example, develop a good strategic plan to keep the organization alive and thriving; develop and play a role in health policy, especially where reimbursement is concerned from federal and state programs; and so on.

TIP

Budgeting can lead to numerous benefits, but none can be realized unless there is total commitment at all levels of management within the organization. The organization can achieve this commitment only by working as a team. Communication is essential to this process. Senior level management must be transparent in creating a culture of fiscal awareness in which information about expenses and revenues is shared. Everyone on the team must work together to forge a strong partnership between organizational, clinical, and financial experts.

For nurse managers specifically, budgeting offers these benefits:

- It forces the nurse manager to think ahead.
- It compels the nurse manager to make choices.
- It provides a plan or forecast of what is expected.
- It provides for communication within the organization.
- It provides a basis for evaluation and control.
- It helps clarify accountability and responsibility.

TIP

Remember: People, not computers, make the budget work.

Financial Variance Monitoring

Financial variance monitoring is a critical aspect of budgeting. It consists of a defined process to evaluate and compare actual operational expenses with budgeted expenses for the same period. (This can be biweekly, monthly, quarterly, or annually.) Should the organization identify a difference, or variance, it can implement appropriate strategies in a timely manner to rectify it.

The Integral Nature of Budgeting

Budgeting is an integral part of the management of any organization. Specifically, budgeting is used in conjunction with the following phases:

- **Planning:** Budgeting is used in the planning phase—that is, in assessing needs and setting future goals. In this phase it is important to understand the organizational priorities. There are two main forms of planning:
    - **Strategic planning:** This type of planning deals with how overall goals are to be met. It does not deal with future decisions

but rather with future implications of today's decisions. Poor financial decisions today will have a negative impact on strategic planning and goals in the future. Likewise, good financial decisions today can enable the organization to proceed with future plans—for example, new services.

- **Tactical planning:** This type of planning involves a series of one-year plans designed to assist the organization in achieving its strategic goals in a prudent and timely manner. Organizations generally develop strategic plans for a three- to five-year period. Strategy involves costs. These costs must be planned in advance for the organization to be able to meet financial commitments in the future.

- **Monitoring:** In this phase, which involves resource allocation, management identifies activities for realizing goals established during the planning phase. For example, suppose a nurse manager recognizes that staff nurses are spending a minimum of two hours doing shift reports. This contributes to a significant amount of overtime, which the organization cannot afford. The nurse manager might then decide to implement walking shift reports at the patients' bedside, which drastically reduces the amount of time spent on shift reports. The result is that overtime decreases and the unit functions more efficiently.
- **Controlling:** Significant variances should trigger further analysis and corrective action. This requires timely reporting and action. Nurse managers need to get comfortable with variance analysis at the time that budget reports are received and reviewed. This is done so that corrective action can take place prior to the next budget cycle. In other words, when negative budget variances exist (that is, when expenses exceed revenues), nurse managers must be able to identify

the contributing factors. The following contributing factors result in the vast majority of variances:

- Increased patient volume
- Inefficiency at the unit level—for example, the unit is overstaffed for volume
- Staffing costs—for example, overtime is used too much or orientation time is not charged to the correct budget line
- Change in patient acuity level—for example, the increased needs of patients during the COVID-19 pandemic and/or the increased need for supplies like PPE

Interview With a Nurse Manager of an Emergency Department

Al had the opportunity to interview a nurse manager of an ED. Constructing a budget for an ED is similar to constructing other departmental budgets, except that staffing and hours—being based on visits rather than nursing hours per patient day—will differ.

Q. *How is revenue generated in an ED?*

A. Revenue varies depending on the type of insurance a patient has (or does not have).

Q. *What are nursing hours based on?*

A. Nursing hours are based on average visit hours in the ED. For reference, the average visit hours for this ED was 2.57 hours. The 2020 average for another ED in the same healthcare system was 2.27 hours. It is also important to understand what is included in those hours. For example, does this include transport, unit secretaries, or other personnel besides registered nurses?

Q. ***What staffing model does your ED use?***

A. This ED uses minimum, average, and maximum staffing models. The staffing model employs RNs, techs (some of whom are LPNs), and unit clerks. ED volume is tracked in an ongoing manner, with peak hours being 11 a.m. to 11 p.m. The ED schedules varied shift hours. These are as follows:

- There are 10 staff members on shift from 7 a.m. to 7 p.m.
- There is one staff member on shift from 9 a.m. to 5 p.m. (This person works five days per week.)
- There are three staff members on shift from 11 a.m. to 11 p.m.
- There are three staff members on shift from 12 p.m. to 12 a.m.
- There are 11 staff members on shift from 7 p.m. to 7 a.m.

Finally, the nurse-to-patient ratio is 1:4.

Q. ***Have any other types of services, such as clinics or urgent care, reduced ED volume?***

A. The Complete Care Clinic has not significantly decreased ED non-emergent volume and is back-logged with appointments. As a result, the ED still sees a lot of primary care patients. Similarly, urgent care has not helped decrease non-emergent volume, as patients must be self-pay or have insurance to go to urgent care. Fortunately, this ED has a dedicated geriatric ED, which has improved care to elderly patients and their families. This geriatric ED even has padding on the floor to prevent serious injury if a patient falls.

Q. ***What effect has COVID-19 had on the ED?***

A. The effects of COVID-19 on this ED have been considerable. There was a 40% reduction in ED volume, but acuity increased. COVID-19 overburdened the ICU but not the ED. An outside tent was erected but was not needed.

Q. ***What does the future of nursing look like for the ED?***

A. There could be a nursing shortage, and having a BSN requirement secondary to Magnet® status may affect the recruitment of staff. Some organizations hire only BSN-prepared nurses, while others hire AND-prepared nurses. Magnet status requires a specific percentage of BSN-prepared nurses; policies related to this are unique to each organization.

–Al Rundio

Summary

This chapter covered:

- The budgeting process for nurse managers and its relationship to patient care
- Nonprofit versus for-profit healthcare organizations
- Other care settings
- What a budget is
- The benefits of budgeting
- The integral nature of budgeting

"Used correctly, a budget doesn't restrict you, it empowers you."

–Tere Stouffer

References

American Hospital Association. (2026). *Fast facts on U.S. hospitals, 2026.* https://www.aha.org/statistics/fast-facts-us-hospitals

Cass, A. (2025, Feb. 25). HCA hospitals by state. *Becker's Hospital Review.* https://www.beckershospitalreview.com/finance/hca-hospitals-by-state-2/#:~:text=Nashville%2C%20Tenn.,Virginia:%2011

Congress.gov. (2024). *Legal requirements for section 501(c)(3) hospitals.* https://www.congress.gov/crs-product/R48027

Hart, R. (2023, July 18). *Organizational types: For-profit and nonprofit.* Management Library. https://management.org/organizations/types.htm

HCA Healthcare. (2026). *Our history.* https://www.hcahealthcare.com/about/our-history

Jones, C. B., Finkler, S. A., Kovner, C. T., & Mose, J. N. (2018). *Financial management for nurse managers and executives* (5th ed.). W. B. Saunders.

Healthcare Reimbursement

To effectively budget, nurse managers must understand how revenue from providing healthcare services is generated. Normally, when you purchase something—whether it's food at the grocery store, a new pair of shoes, or a car—you provide payment for that item at the time of purchase. With healthcare, however, things work a bit differently. Typically, when someone receives healthcare services, payment for those services is rendered later, either by the person's insurance company, through government health programs, or out of the patient's pocket. This is known as *reimbursement*. Reimbursement is all of the money a healthcare organization earns from its operations, including the services that are provided to patients. This comes from insurers (Medicaid, Medicare, commercial insurance companies), patient out of pocket payments, and value-based incentive payments. A healthcare facility's reimbursements represent the bulk of its revenue.

This chapter will focus on reimbursements and provide an overview of political factors, historical and current, that affect healthcare policies and processes in the United States, including reimbursement. The chapter then outlines the history of healthcare reimbursement in the US, covering the following topics:

- Per diem reimbursement
- Diagnosis-related groups (DRGs)
- Medicare and Medicaid
- Managed care
- Health maintenance organizations (HMOs)
- Preferred provider organizations (PPOs)
- Capitation
- Accountable care organizations (ACOs)

"The best investment you can make is in yourself. The more you learn, the more you earn."

–Warren Buffett

It is important for nurses to understand both the political context and the history of healthcare reimbursement in the US. Unlike the vast majority of countries in Europe, which have single-payer healthcare systems, the US has a market-driven entrepreneurial healthcare system that relies heavily on private markets, private insurers, and employer-based insurance coverage. This creates fragmentation, with different people receiving care through different mechanisms and no single structure. Legislation at both the federal and state level has shaped healthcare reimbursement in the US. Gaining an understanding of where and when healthcare reimbursement began is critical to understanding where healthcare is today, and more importantly, where it is going in the future.

US Healthcare: A Political Primer

Healthcare policy and financing are intricately intertwined. For example, in Europe and most Eastern countries, healthcare is a politically won universal right, with the government being the major guarantor of reimbursement. In the US, however, the political consensus has traditionally favored a market-based approach to healthcare financing, with the individual being responsible to pay for care—either personally or through third-party arrangements with employer-provided healthcare plans or directly with insurers. Public sentiment and political will in the US have resulted in a diversion from a pure market-based approach when it comes to some vulnerable populations and healthcare reimbursement. The elderly and disabled are covered by federal funds allocated to Medicare. Low-income persons are covered by a mix of federal and state funds allocated to Medicaid. Both Medicaid and Medicare are discussed later in this chapter. However, healthcare costs include more than just the dollar amount of care. For those who do not have insurance, Medicare and Medicaid can have social costs as well due to loss of individual income and decreased productivity due to illness, and poorer overall health and shorter life expectancy as a result of lack of access to healthcare.

To better understand healthcare reimbursement, it helps to know the general political history of healthcare in the US. This section reviews that history from about 1929 to the current day. It provides an overview of how insurance plans began to develop. The early formation of such plans has provided a foundation for the type of healthcare delivery system and financing that exists today.

1929 to 1940

Before World War II, there were partially funded care-delivery systems. For example, when Blue Cross was initiated, only inpatient hospital care was funded. Outpatient care, such as a physician office visit and prescription medication, was not funded. Some employers provided onsite medical care for workers, with the rationale that worker productivity would thus be secure. This setup was not considered an employee benefit.

Issues that affected healthcare policy, delivery, and cost prior to World War II included the growth and expansion of science and technology and developments in trauma care. In addition, infectious diseases were still prevalent because antibiotics were in their infancy.

In Europe, the move toward "socialized" medicine, or universal coverage via compulsory and nationalized health insurance, started before World War I. By the late 1930s, nearly every Central European and Eastern country had government-sponsored healthcare for employees and the disadvantaged. The US did not follow this trend.

A major turning point in the American healthcare system occurred in 1929. That year was the beginning of the Great Depression. The Great Depression devastated the healthcare system by making care unaffordable, increasing deaths from preventable causes, and causing financial hardship for providers. It also spurned crucial reforms that accelerated the privatization of healthcare coverage in the US, originally as prepaid single-hospital service plans. Within 10 years, prepaid-premium plans with the Blue Cross designation were replicated in every state. Legislatures, physician groups, and healthcare institutions supported these plans. As a means of survival as finances became unstable, hospitals increasingly started accepting reimbursement from insurance companies. Because Blue Cross was the predominant insurer nationwide, hospitals began to seek their certification as a way to attract patients whose bills would certainly be paid. To attain Blue Cross designation, hospitals agreed to reduce price competition and to allow subscribers free choice of hospital and provider. This severely undermined single-hospital prepaid plans.

The 1930s are considered the development era of healthcare financing. During this period, healthcare policy and funding continued to change. Parallel development of prepaid group practices occurred. The popularity of prepaid medical care plans increased. Some healthcare providers balked at these changes, though. Even legislative action was invoked against consumer-run medical plans.

Blue Shield plans were developed during this period. These plans provided reimbursement specifically for physician services. The impetus for Blue Shield plans was physicians' fear of losing their practice autonomy—including diagnoses, schedule of care, and most importantly, their own fees—and the sanctity of the physician-patient relationship, based on the belief that insurance-accepting hospitals might start covering physician services under such plans.

1941 to 1964

After the US entered World War II in 1941, more and more employers began to offer health insurance as an incentive or benefit to recruit and retain staff. Insurers benefited because these employee groups were less likely to be ill than older individuals not in the employment sector. Administrative costs were low because it was the working well who enrolled in the plans. Most of the insured were covered by Blue Cross plans.

NOTE

Employer-sponsored group healthcare programs began to proliferate during the 1940s. One reason that employers increasingly offered these plans was that US government–mandated wage freezes during the war years meant that employers could not offer higher wages as a way to attract and retain workers. Instead, they offered group healthcare programs as part of their benefits packages (Preskitt, 2008).

Post–World War II aspects of healthcare included a higher quality of life and increasing life expectancy. Labor unions had a major impact on healthcare coverage during this period. In 1948, the Supreme Court held that health insurance fell within the "conditions of employment" and was thus within the purview of union negotiation and collective bargaining (Justia, n.d.). Unions paid a lot of attention to healthcare plans and fostered the development of employer-sponsored (or direct service) plans.

Unrestricted access to healthcare resulted in cost inflation. In the 1950s, more than 60% of the population had healthcare insurance. Employers generally paid more than 35% of healthcare premiums for their employees and more than 20% for employee dependents (Preskitt, 2008). Meanwhile, the country lacked a national healthcare policy. There was resistance to restrictions on any part of the healthcare delivery system. Blue Cross at this time guaranteed full payment for services rendered, especially if the patient was treated in an inpatient hospital setting.

1965

1965 was a pivotal year for healthcare. It was when Lyndon B. Johnson, then President of the US, implemented two new social programs that former President John F. Kennedy had been working on: Medicare and Medicaid. Medicare was meant to insure the elderly and special populations such as dialysis patients. Medicaid was designed to cover the working poor. The implementation of Medicare and Medicaid represented an expanded role of government in financing and organizing the healthcare delivery system in the US.

1980s

The 1980s saw a proliferation of health maintenance organizations (HMOs) and prepaid group plans. These provided cost controls by having the primary care physician serve as a "gatekeeper" controlling access to other services like specialists, diagnostic tests, and hospital care. HMOs often maintained their own hospitals and clinics or made payment arrangements with specific hospitals and providers. They also employed their own physician staff and other staff members. HMOs removed the fee-for-service incentive from providers. They also kept rates of use low—including the use of advanced medical technology.

The Debate Over National Health Insurance

There is an ongoing healthcare debate in the US that has frequently influenced healthcare policy, has stalled at other times, and has recently become a topic that initiates lively discussion at political rallies (to say nothing of family get-togethers): national health insurance.

National health insurance has been the subject of debate in the US for decades, beginning in the 1930s. At that time, President Franklin D. Roosevelt favored the passage of the Social Security Bill of 1935 but feared that including a compulsory national health insurance component in that bill or passing it as a separate piece of legislation might doom passage of Social Security. In 1943, the Wagner-Murray-Dingel Bill was introduced in Congress. This bill proposed a national health plan to insure every American citizen. The bill was defeated in 1950 after fierce opposition by the American Medical Association (AMA). The AMA believed the bill would result in the enslavement of the medical profession.

The 1950s and 1960s brought a resurgence of public discussion about a national healthcare plan. In the 1980s, Senator Edward Kennedy of Massachusetts kept the issue of a national healthcare plan in the headlines. In the 1990s, a discussion about a national healthcare plan again dominated headlines. This latter discussion occurred under President Bill Clinton's administration during the first 100 days of his presidency, when he appointed his wife, Hillary Rodham Clinton, to develop a national health plan. This bill was also defeated.

In 2010, Congress passed the Patient Protection and Affordable Care Act (ACA), which President Barack Obama signed into law. The ACA seeks to insure American citizens who, before the act, were either uninsurable (for example, because of a preexisting condition) or uninsured (usually because they could not afford the premiums due to their lower economic status).

Most recently, in 2016 and 2020, some presidential candidates proposed a Medicare for All plan during their campaigns. In the 2024 presidential campaign, both President Joe Biden and Vice President and then presidential candidate Kamala Harris campaigned on expanding Medicare to add additional benefits, including home healthcare.

2003

The Medicare Drug, Improvement, and Modernization Act of 2003 (aka the Medicare Modernization Act of 2003, or the MMA) amends Title XVIII of the Social Security Act. This landmark overhaul of the Medicare program provided for a voluntary prescription drug benefit under the Medicare program to strengthen and improve the Medicare program.

The MMA made Medicare prescription drug plans available beginning in January 2006. This is called Medicare Part D. It was designed to protect individuals from high out-of-pocket costs. It pays part of the cost of covered prescription drugs. This plan is available for all people with Medicare and is provided through private prescription drug plans, Medicare Advantage plans, and some employers and unions for retirees. Enrollment is voluntary. To be eligible to enroll in the plan, an individual had to be entitled to Part A of Medicare and enrolled in Part B of Medicare. (These are discussed in more detail later in the chapter.)

NOTE

Why would someone want to join a prescription drug plan? Medical practices incorporate new drug therapies to treat chronic conditions, and this practice is increasing. Out-of-pocket spending on drugs has increased. As people age, it is more likely they will need prescription drugs to remain healthy.

From 2010 to Today

In recent years, in addition to access and quality, one of the driving forces behind healthcare delivery has been cost control. Generally, when a new business is started, the cost line increases as well as the quality line. After the business is operational for a while, the quality line usually increases, and the cost line levels off or lowers. In the US, when it comes to healthcare, the opposite has traditionally occurred. The cost line continues to rise, and the quality line lowers—the complete opposite of what *should* happen. These increased costs stem from higher administrative fees and the increasing cost of technology and pharmaceuticals. Indeed, these two factors alone result in US healthcare expenses that far exceed those of other nations.

As mentioned, the Patient Protection and ACA, passed in 2010, seeks to insure American citizens who before the act were either uninsurable or uninsured. The act also addresses quality and cost.

NOTE

The American Academy of Medicine, previously known as the Institute of Medicine, has also been a major player in trying to improve quality in the US healthcare delivery system.

The ACA calls for the use of ACOs. An ACO consists of a *medical home*, which is usually a primary care physician or a clinic. The purpose of the medical home is to provide oversight for patients, wherever they are in the healthcare system—in other words, disease management. ACOs use value-based purchasing to judiciously manage both quality of care and cost; providers who provide excellent care receive increased payments. This means asking the following questions:

- What value is assured to the patient?
- What value is the patient receiving by purchasing a certain organization's healthcare services?

For example, suppose a hospital has one guaranteed price, regardless of outcome. So, if a patient were to undergo open heart surgery at that hospital and later develop a surgical wound infection requiring readmission, there would be no additional charge to the patient or the insurance company. In such an organization, if quality problems regularly occur, payment is reduced. This creates an incentive for them to improve quality so they will be paid more. This practice, along with bundled billing, enables ACOs to demonstrate significant cost savings with improved quality of care to the patient.

NOTE

Quality must exist throughout any service offered in an ACO.

Home care is another critical component of an ACO. Insurance companies will pay for home care services because generally these services are less costly than hospital admissions and can even prevent hospital admissions and readmissions.

NOTE

For a more detailed discussion on home care, see Chapter 11. For more on the ACA, see Chapter 9.

Issues Driving Continued Changes in Healthcare Policy and Funding

Issues that will continue to drive changes to healthcare policy and the funding in healthcare include:

- The growing elderly population
- Fewer caregivers
- An aging educational workforce
- An aging healthcare workforce
- More retired individuals tapping Social Security and Medicare
- A variety of practice settings
- Advances in technology (for example, telehealth services)
- Emerging pandemics

Healthcare Reimbursement in the United States

There are several types of healthcare reimbursement in the US. This section covers these—including some that are no longer widely in use.

Bad Debt

Sometimes, healthcare facilities receive no reimbursement for care given. There are two main reasons for this:

- **The patient cannot pay:** Many Americans are uninsured, which means they are unable to afford care they receive. Even some Americans who are insured may not be able to afford to pay their co-pays and deductibles—a situation exacerbated by the recession that began in 2008, the one that occurred as a result of COVID-19 starting in 2020, and the general economic climate.
- **The insurance provider denies payment or only partially pays a claim:** Sometimes, the insurance provider claims that care given was not medically necessary or that a patient's continued stay was not medically required. Or they might blame the healthcare facility for an iatrogenic event (a medical problem resulting from the fault of the provider) that resulted in the patient staying longer. In both cases, the insurance provider might refuse to reimburse the healthcare facility.

Medical bills that a hospital, clinic, or healthcare provider expected to be paid but ultimately cannot collect is referred to as *bad debt*. Bad debt is written off as a financial loss.

Charity Care

Care that is free or discounted and given to patients who cannot afford to pay or meet financial need criteria is *charity care*. Healthcare facilities and providers intentionally provide the care without expecting partial or full payment. Charity care is often provided as part of an organization's mission.

Per Diem and Self-Pay Reimbursement

In the 1970s, reimbursement was most often based on a per diem rate, paid by insurers. A *per diem rate* is a daily fee or rate that is billed and paid. Thus, hospitals were simply reimbursed whatever they charged. In the 1970s, the payer was typically Blue Cross and Blue Shield, Medicare, or Medicaid.

Hospitals charged a per diem rate for hospital services. Such rates were generally calculated by averaging daily expenses incurred over the entire hospital census. Per diem rates were usually reviewed and approved by hospital rate-setting commissions in each state. These commissions were established through the respective state's legislative process.

The other form of reimbursement during this period was *self-pay reimbursement*. With this type of reimbursement, the patient paid for what was billed. Al provides a personal example: "In 1970, when my first child was born, he had a congenital hernia that needed repair. Because at that time I did not have a job that provided health insurance, I set up a payment plan with the hospital, to which I made a monthly payment until the bill was paid in full."

Under both these systems, hospitals had no incentive to discharge patients early because they basically were paid what they billed. By the latter part of the 1970s, however, insurance providers began to question generous reimbursements to hospitals. In an effort to control healthcare costs, these companies introduced the diagnosis-related groups (DRG) system. This was a system of averages. Rather than paying a daily rate, insurance companies using the DRG system paid a case rate, which was identified by a particular code. Under this system, which was adopted nationally under Medicare, insurance companies began to control healthcare costs. For the first time, hospitals had an incentive to discharge patients early.

NOTE

Providers quickly learned their way around the DRG system to maximize reimbursements. They did this by using DRG coders to review medical records in detail and code them such that reimbursements could be increased.

Third-party payers, like insurance companies (discussed next), also began negotiating for discount rates. The difference between the amount charged and the amount paid under these discount rates was known as the *contractual allowance.*

The Early Role of Insurance Companies

Insurance companies were originally devised to cover acute care hospitalization. Initially, the main insurance company in the US was Blue Cross and Blue Shield. During the 1970s, this company covered inpatient hospitalization services far more than outpatient services. For example, one plan Al had covered $25 for outpatient care for an entire family for a one-year time period. However, if the patient was admitted to the hospital, all procedures were covered.

NOTE

Patients were often admitted to acute care hospitals for testing procedures even though such procedures could be completed in an outpatient setting. This was because patients would have been responsible for most of the charges had the procedures been performed on an outpatient basis.

The Advent of Medicare and Medicaid

As noted, to provide insurance for the elderly, disabled, and other poor or vulnerable populations, the US government, under President Lyndon B. Johnson, implemented Medicare and Medicaid. Medicare covers individuals ages 65 and up. It also covers individuals under the age of 65 if they have certain disabilities—for example, if someone is on renal dialysis or requires a renal transplant for end-stage renal disease (Medicare.gov, n.d.).

Medicaid is a US government health insurance program that helps pay for medical care for people with low income or limited resources. It mainly covers low-income adults, children, pregnant women, and people with disabilities. Eligibility depends on income, household size, and state rules because each state runs its own Medicaid program within federal guidelines.

NOTE

Persons who use Medicare must reside in the US.

Medicare consists of four parts:

- **Part A:** This covers inpatient care in hospitals, skilled nursing facilities (SNFs), critical access hospitals (small facilities that give limited outpatient and inpatient services to people in rural areas), and hospice care, and provides care for specific patient populations (for example, dialysis patients). Medicare Part A covers 100% of the first 20 days in an SNF if:
    - The patient was previously admitted to an acute care hospital for a minimum of three consecutive inpatient days. However, under certain circumstances, this minimum may be waived, such as if the facility is an ACO or the patient's Medicare Advantage plan has lesser requirements (CMS.gov, n.d.-b; Medicare.gov, n.d.).
    - The patient entered the SNF within a short time (generally 30 days) of leaving a hospital (CMS.gov, n.d.-c; Medicare.gov, n.d.).

- After the 20 days in the SNF, Medicare Part A covers days 21–100 in the facility at $217 a day (see Table 2.1).

TABLE 2.1 MEDICARE PART A COVERAGE IN A NURSING HOME

Medicare Days Covered	Amount Paid by Medicare	Amount Paid by Resident
Days 1 to 20	100%	$0
Days 21 to 100	$217 a day	The remaining balance
Days 100 and beyond	0%	100%

CMS.gov, n.d.-b; Medicare.gov, n.d.

- **Part B:** This covers outpatient care, such as physician office visits, durable medical equipment, physical therapy, home healthcare, and other services such as screenings, vaccines, and yearly wellness visits.
- **Part C:** This is a Medicare Advantage plan, much like an HMO or a PPO (discussed later in the chapter). A Medicare Advantage plan bundles together Part A, Part B, and Part D coverage and offers some extra benefits that original Medicare does not. Medicare Advantage plans are offered by private companies approved by Medicare. Those who join a Medicare Advantage plan have all the rights and protections guaranteed by the Medicare program and obtain all regular Medicare-covered services. In addition, they may be eligible for extra benefits such as coverage for extra days in a hospital (CMS.gov, n.d.-a).

NOTE

Private fee-for-service plans and specialty plans are also available in some states.

- **Part D:** This is an optional prescription drug plan, offered by private insurance companies approved by Medicare. Initially enacted in 2005 under President George W. Bush, individuals paid an additional premium of about $37 per month with a yearly deductible of up to $250. (Enhanced benefits cost more.) To be eligible to enroll in the plan, an individual had to be entitled to Part A of Medicare and enrolled in Part B of Medicare (Megellas, 2006). Over time the program has changed to reduce costs of coverage gaps (often referred to as the "donut hole"), provide expanded protections for preventive medications, add real protection against unlimited costs, and fully eliminate the donut hole with greater responsibility shifted to plans and drug manufacturers.

The Part D "Donut Hole"

When enacted, the Part D plan covered up to $2,700 per year. If patients' prescription costs were higher than that, they were responsible for paying the difference themselves until they hit $7,050. At that point, the plan would pick up again and continue to cover costs. This gap was called the *donut hole*. One of the provisions of the ACA was to close the donut hole over a period of years, finishing in 2020 (Medicare Rights Center, 2025). As of 2025, the Medicare Part D donut hole no longer exists. Beneficiaries pay nothing for covered prescriptions after reaching the annual $2,000 total out-of-pocket cap (National Council on Aging, 2026).

The administrative department of the federal government that oversees these programs is called the Centers for Medicare & Medicaid Services (CMS).

Patients with Medicare have rights. These include the following (CMS.gov, n.d.-a):

- Obtaining information about all treatment choices
- Participating in treatment decisions
- Obtaining easy-to-understand information
- Knowing which costs are paid by Medicare and which costs they have to pay
- Receiving emergency department services
- Having their personal health information kept secure and private
- Not facing discrimination on the basis of race, color, national origin, disability, age, gender, sexual orientation, or religion

NOTE

Patients with Alzheimer's disease enrolled in the Medicare program have the same rights and coverage that any other person has with Medicare.

Patients with Medicare also have the right to information about filing an appeal or grievance. Such appeals can be filed when:

- Medicare does not make payment
- Medicare does not pay enough
- The patient is not provided with the service covered under Medicare

NOTE

Generally, grievances relate to quality-of-care issues (CMS.gov, 2024).

Managed Care

In the early 1990s, as healthcare costs increased, insurance companies ushered in managed care. *Managed care* describes any system that manages healthcare delivery with the goal of controlling costs.

Managed-care systems typically incorporate a primary-care base. Primary care functions as a gatekeeper through which the patient must pass to obtain other health services, such as specialty medical care, surgery, or physical therapy.

Some of the key elements of managed care include the following:

- Selective contracting
- Price competition
- Creation of integrated health networks
- Emergence of large physician groups
- Dominance of insurance companies
- Geographic growth of for-profit institutions

The outcomes in managed care are achieved through decreased lengths of hospital stays, denial of certain procedures, case management and critical pathways, minimally invasive procedures, the bundling of services and payment, capitation, and a focus on patient outcomes, both from a physical standpoint and a quality-of-care standpoint.

NOTE

The managed-care model has definitely controlled costs through the control of procedures and hospital admissions.

Why the Rising Costs?

Healthcare costs rise for many reasons. One is an increase in labor costs. Another is that advances in technology bring new types of care that involve increased costs. In addition, pharmaceutical costs continue to rise, as do malpractice insurance premiums for providers. The aging population and increase in chronic disease require ongoing expensive treatment.

Today, there are five main kinds of managed care products:

- **Health maintenance organizations (HMOs):** The purpose of this type of managed-care product was (and is) to focus on the promotion of health and the prevention of illness. Primary care, women's health services, and other such services are generally reimbursed under HMOs. When participating in an HMO, patients select a primary care provider; the primary care provider coordinates the patient's care and then refers the patient to specialists as needed. Coverage is limited to in-network providers (except for emergencies). This type of product provides lower premiums and out-of-pocket costs with an emphasis on preventive care. However, choice is limited, and referrals are required for specialty care.
- **Preferred provider organizations (PPOs):** A PPO, sometimes referred to as a *participating provider organization,* is essentially a managed-care organization of medical doctors, hospitals, and other healthcare providers who have covenanted with an insurer or a third-party administrator to provide healthcare at reduced rates to the insurer's or administrator's clients. In a PPO, patients are referred by the insurance company to preferred providers with whom the company has a contract. A primary care physician is not required, and patients can see out-of-network providers but at a higher cost.

- **Point-of-service plans (POSs):** This type of managed-care plan has characteristics of both an HMO and a PPO and offers more flexibility. In a POS plan, the patient selects a primary care provider from a list of participating providers. All medical care is directed by this provider—that is, the provider is the patient's "point of service." The provider makes referrals to other in-network providers should a specialist be needed. There is a broad base of medical providers in the POS network, which typically covers a large geographic area.
- **Independent provider associations (IPAs):** Some physicians may form an IPA within a particular specialty or primary care workgroup. An IPA, also referred to as an *independent practice association*, is an association of independent physicians or other organizations that contracts with independent physicians. Services are provided to managed-care organizations on a negotiated per-capita rate, flat retainer fee, or negotiated fee-for-service basis. An HMO or other managed-care plan may contract with an IPA, which in turn contracts with independent physicians to treat members at discounted fees or on a capitation basis.
- **High-deductible health plans:** This type of insurance plan has a higher annual deductible (the amount a patient pays before insurance starts covering most services) and lower monthly premiums compared to traditional plans. Preventive services are generally covered 100% and are often good for healthy individuals with few medical visits. However, the financial risk is greater if unexpected illness occurs.

Capitation

In its simplest form, *capitation* is a set reimbursement that is applied regardless of how many times a patient accesses a provider. For example, with capitation, which evolved during the 1990s, an insurance company might reimburse a primary care provider $10 per month for each patient, regardless of whether a patient sees the provider once per month, five times per month, or not at all. The payment covers a defined set of services regardless of how frequently the patient uses those services.

There are six basic types of capitation:

- **Partnership capitation:** In this model, the physician and the hospital to which the physician refers patients work collaboratively. The goal is cost-effective care, both in the provider's office and at the hospital (if a patient requires hospitalization).
- **Network capitation:** An example of this type of capitation would be a healthcare organization that owns multiple acute care hospitals. All these hospitals would be in a capitated model with a particular insurance plan.
- **System capitation:** An example of this type of capitation would be a hospital system that owns more than just acute care hospitals. For example, the hospital system might own several acute care hospitals, long-term care facilities, and assisted-living facilities and offer access to pharmaceuticals, durable medical equipment, outpatient physical therapy, and home care. A patient in a capitated plan would be capitated across the system.
- **Chronic disease capitation:** This describes the capitation of care for certain chronic illnesses, such as diabetes, HIV infection, heart failure, and other such illnesses. With this type of capitation, rather than an insurance company reimbursing every diagnosis, only certain chronic illness diagnoses would be capitated.
- **Carve-out capitation:** An example of carve-out capitation would be an insurance company that carves out certain diagnoses that are not chronic in nature and capitates them—for example, cataract surgery, total joint surgery, and other such nonchronic illnesses.
- **Medicare capitation:** An example of this type of capitation would be the Medicare program reimbursing acute care hospitals under a capitated model rather than the DRG system.

If you were to compare proposed insurance models, capitation would save the most money. In a capitated model, risks for patient care are shared both by the provider and the insurance carrier, with the vast majority of risk being taken by the provider.

Program of All-Inclusive Care for the Elderly (PACE)

Another example of a Medicare capitated model of payment is care rendered in a Program of All-Inclusive Care for the Elderly (PACE) center (CMS.gov, 2026b). PACE centers are administered by CMS.

The primary purpose of a PACE center is to meet the needs of the elderly within the community rather than at facilities such as nursing homes. The goal of a PACE center is to provide quality care and to treat patients so that inpatient acute care will not be necessary. At times, some patients may remain enrolled in a PACE center even if they have been admitted to a nursing home and receive care there as well.

PACE centers are reimbursed with a capitated rate per member per month. Care is rendered by a team of providers in medicine, nursing, occupational therapy, physical therapy, mental health, social work, and discharge planning. Patients attend the program every weekday. In addition, patients may receive care at home.

The COVID-19 pandemic had a profound effect on PACE centers. These facilities had to limit the number of patients in each center to maintain social distancing. To achieve this, they have begun providing care on a rotation basis, as well as conducting more home visits. As a result of learning from the COVID-19 pandemic, PACE centers have now implemented innovative technology to better provide services in infectious disease surges and emergency operations, such as limiting contact with a computerized reminder system that reminds patients to take their medication at a set time.

The Role of Philanthropy

When an individual or an organization makes a philanthropic financial donation to a healthcare facility such as a hospital, that donation constitutes non-operating revenue support. Philanthropic donations can assist organizations in providing care. Many philanthropic organizations donate large sums of money, often in exchange for the hospital naming a program or portion of a building after the donor.

NOTE

Some donors who make financial contributions place restrictions on their use. These are called *restricted resources.* With restricted resources, the donor earmarks the area in which the donation should be applied (hospice, cardiac care, pediatric facilities, etc.).

Some of the most powerful donations are those from grateful patients. These gifts are made to express gratitude for care received or to honor a specific doctor, nurse, or department.

Types of Healthcare Reimbursement: A Summary

Table 2.2 summarizes the various types of reimbursement in the US for the provision of healthcare.

TABLE 2.2 METHODS OF REIMBURSEMENT

Type of Reimbursement	Explanation
Per diem rate	This involves the payment of a billable daily rate.
Self-pay	In this model, the individual pays for care.

continues

TABLE 2.2 METHODS OF REIMBURSEMENT (CONT.)

Type of Reimbursement	Explanation
Medicare	This is a federal system of reimbursement that consists of four parts: A (acute care hospitalization and nursing home reimbursement); B (outpatient care—for example, physical therapy; primary care office visits); C (Medicare Advantage plans); and D (prescription drug plan). Medicare pays a fixed amount per inpatient, based on the discharge diagnosis.
Medicaid	Title XIX, which called for the formation of Medicaid, was enacted in 1965 by President Lyndon B. Johnson. Medicaid provides insurance for the poor. The federal government and states share in costs. Medicaid usually pays less than stated charges, with the amount varying from state to state.
Managed care	Managed-care plans represent an effort by insurance companies to control costs and balance quality.
HMO	The focus of HMOs is on primary care and prevention.
PPO	With a PPO, the insurance company contracts with certain providers.
IPA	An IPA is an association of independent physicians or other organizations that contracts with independent physicians. Services are provided to managed-care organizations.
Capitation	This is a set reimbursement that is applied regardless of how many times a patient accesses a provider. For example, an insurance company might reimburse a primary care provider $10 per month, regardless of whether a patient sees the provider once per month, five times per month, or none at all.
Philanthropy	Considered non-operating revenue support, not reimbursement. In this model, funds are received from donors.
Charity care	Most healthcare institutions provide some amount of charity care, or free care. Some states have a charity care pool or fund; these funds typically reimburse hospitals that offer the most charity care. Often, community hospitals receive little or no payment for charity care.

Turning a Positive Financial Line

It is very challenging for most hospitals and providers to turn a positive financial line on operations. In recent years, reimbursement rates from managed care and federal, state, and other insurance programs have not kept pace with expenses for salaries, benefits, supplies, and general operations. In addition, not-for-profit hospitals must take any profit that is made and use it to fund new purchases of equipment and for facility repairs, often referred to as capital expenses. Think about it: If a hospital has a 2% positive line on operations on, say, a $100 million budget, the hospital has turned a profit of $2 million. That might sound like a lot of money, but in today's world, it is not. In most hospitals, one bad month could result in the loss of that $2 million profit.

Reimbursement for Long-Term Care

There are several different types of long-term care, including nursing homes or SNFs, assisted living facilities, adult day care, and home-based care. Reimbursement for long-term care is different from hospital care. Long-term care is usually paid for by Medicare or Medicaid, through long-term care insurance or out of a person's pocket (self-pay).

NOTE

There are federal guidelines under the Medicare program related to reimbursement for long-term care (National Council on Aging, 2026). Each state has different guidelines regarding Medicaid, private insurances, and self-payments.

Skilled Nursing Facilities

Services in an SNF are provided based on a comprehensive resident assessment known as the *Minimum Data Set,* 3rd Edition (MDS 3.0). This assessment establishes a score based on the resident's needs. From this information, a formula is used to calculate the reimbursement rate. A case mix index number is also created from this data. In general, the higher the case mix index score, the higher the reimbursement. Examples of scenarios that might increase a case mix index score include residents requiring daily assistance with the activities of daily living or intense physical or speech therapy.

In an SNF, nursing hours per patient day generally start at two hours per day and increase based on acuity. For example, a resident with a feeding tube would have increased nursing care hours per patient day. Of course, the more patients and nursing hours per patient day, the more care providers are needed. Because many nursing homes now have subacute nursing units, some states require a minimum of one RN on each shift. A typical RN-to-resident ratio would be 1 RN to 10 patients on day shift, 1 RN to 15 patients on evening shift, and 1 RN to 20 patients on night shift. SNFs also supplement staff with certified medical assistants. This relates to reimbursement because as the case mix index number increases, reimbursement also increases.

Assisted Living Facilities

Assisted living facilities are reimbursed in a variety of ways:

- Private insurers can establish contracted rates with the facility.
- Medicare Part B can reimburse occupational therapy, physical therapy, and other outpatient services.
- Medicaid can reimburse such facilities in some states.
- Auto insurance can reimburse care in some states (see the sidebar in this section for a story about one such case).

Assisted living facilities use a tiered system based on the intensity of services required. The usual rating is between 1 and 4, with 4 being the highest level. An example of a level 4 resident would be a resident who requires complete care. In general, there are additional fees for levels higher than level 1. If Medicaid or other insurers do not factor in these levels when reimbursing for care, the resident is responsible for these fees.

Assisted living facilities generally have one RN on the day shift. This nurse must be on call 24/7 for any emergency or problem. Nursing assistants certified in medication administration comprise the rest of the staff. Some assisted living facilities maintain round-the-clock nurses—for example, an RN on the day shift and LPNs on the evening and night shifts. The higher the level, the more dollars the facility charges.

Real-World Example From Al Rundio: An Assisted Living Facility Resident's Story

In 1980, my brother-in-law was involved in a motorcycle accident. The extent of his facial and neuro injuries was severe. He was not expected to survive, but he did. He will never be 100%, but he is a functioning member of society and can even work at some jobs. His mother cared for him up until her death.

He was most fortunate in that his motorcycle insurance policy included a provision that it would cover healthcare expenses related to his accident for life. Most insurance companies and policies do not have such provisions today. He required supervised care—for example, making certain he gets his medications on time. His therapist and the case manager for the auto insurance determined that the most effective intervention would be to have him reside in an assisted living facility. This is the facility's first—and right now only—resident whose care is covered by an auto insurance company.

Home Care

Home-based care may include help with daily activities, home health aides or personal care assistants, or skilled nursing visits for wound care, injections, or therapy. It is the least restrictive type of long-term care and is paid for by various means:

- The Outcome and Assessment Information Set (OASIS) program under Medicare
- Some private insurance plans
- Medicaid (in some states)

The OASIS Program

The OASIS program (O'Connor & Davitt, 2012) is a patient-specific, standardized assessment used in Medicare and Medicaid home health care to plan care, determine reimbursement, and measure quality (CMS, 2026a). The tool is required for home health clinicians to evaluate a patient's physical and functional status, measure their progress over time, and determine Medicare reimbursement. OASIS is completed at the start of care, every 65 days for recertification, and any time care is resumed following a hospitalization, transfer, discharge, or death at home. It is not required for patients under age 18, those receiving maternity services, or patients receiving only personal care, housekeeping, or assistance with other chores.

Addiction Rehabilitation Facilities and Services

Rates for addiction rehabilitation facilities and services vary depending on the location; the patient's insurance company; whether the facility is in-network or out-of-network; the duration of the treatment; whether the treatment is residential or outpatient; and even by the type of substance abuse being treated (opioid treatment generally costing more). For facilities that are in-network, the contracted provider is paid an agreed-upon rate. For out-of-network facilities, the patient pays more out of pocket.

NOTE

Patients might choose an out-of-network facility because of unique services it provides—for example, a facility that centers care on holistic interventions.

Each insurance company has its own rates and policies regarding the number of days allowed at an addiction rehabilitation facility, although longer treatment plans are often offered at a discount (National Center for Drug Abuse Statistics, 2025). For reference, typical costs for outpatient treatment at such facilities are:

- **Detox:** Detoxification services are $525 average per day (seven days minimum) for outpatient treatment with insurance; $1,000 average per day (seven days minimum) without insurance
- **Inpatient residential program:** Short-term plans last three to six weeks at an average cost of $42,500. A sober living facility averages $1,500 to $2,000 per month.
- **Inpatient hospital program:** A typical plan is for 28–30 inpatient days, with an average cost of $12,500 for the full treatment plan.
- **Intensive outpatient program:** Per episode, the average cost ranges from $1,908 to $7,969, with many rehab centers offering a three-month program for $5,000. Daily cost averages $575 per day for alcohol rehabilitation, for example.

(National Center for Drug Abuse Statistics, 2025)

NOTE

Since passage of the ACA, which includes substance use services as an essential health insurance benefit, both Medicaid and Medicare cover substance use disorder intervention, treatment, and counseling services and medication. In 2020, Medicaid provided coverage to 21% of non-elderly adults with substance use disorder, or approximately 13.9 million Americans (Saunders & Rudowitz, 2022). Medicare Part A covers medication such as methadone while the patient is in a hospital. Medicare Part B covers substance use disorder treatment, including medication, without cost to the patient if the services are provided by an opioid treatment program enrolled in Medicare. If the services are provided by a doctor or healthcare provider not part of such a program, then the usual copayments after the deductible is met apply (Medicare.gov, n.d.).

The Role of Social Policy

Nurses responsible for budgeting in their organizations must have a general understanding of social policy both at the federal and state levels. This is because healthcare dollars and social policy are intertwined. For example, suppose the federal government changes Medicare reimbursement policies such that patient care providers are reimbursed for less. This could translate to layoffs of personnel in a hospital or other provider setting. As another example, this one at the state level, consider New Jersey, where charity care is funded by the state. If the state's social policy were to reduce charity care funding, each hospital providing charity care would experience a decrease in reimbursement.

Real-World Example From Al Rundio: Political Action

When I was a vice president for nursing in a hospital, the director of education at the same facility was on the board of the New Jersey State Nurses Association political action committee (PAC).

One year, a federal bill was sponsored that would drastically reduce Medicare payments to acute care hospitals. In response, the director of education, also a nurse, staffed tables outside our hospital's cafeteria with volunteers. Anytime an employee visited the cafeteria, a volunteer at the table asked them to read a summary of the proposed legislation and to sign a petition urging our congressional representative to vote against it. Then, another volunteer at the table dialed the congressional representative's office, handed the phone to the employee, and advised the employee to tell the congressional representative's aide to advise the congressman to vote against the legislation.

Within a few days, this congressman had received more than 1,000 pieces of mail and more than 1,000 telephone calls on this issue. Fortunately, he heard the message. Our congressional representative was one of four Republicans who voted against this Republican-sponsored legislation. (Incidentally, this congressional representative was reelected several times because he listened to his constituents and addressed their concerns.)

Complicating matters, thanks to the way our system of government was designed, each state is its own entity, almost like a separate country (hence, the United States of America). So, each state's policies—including those that relate to healthcare—may differ. This becomes evident when one studies how many US Supreme Court decisions defer to decisions made in the respective state. The US response to the COVID-19 pandemic also illustrates the key role that states and social policy play in healthcare delivery.

Nurses as Political Activists

Nurses must be politically active when proposed legislation is moving through the system. Nurses can become politically active in various ways:

- **Becoming a registered voter:** Congressional representatives, senators, and other political figures will not listen to anyone who is not a registered voter. Votes are what put and keep political figures in office.
- **Participating in grassroots efforts:** A simple way to become politically involved is through grassroots efforts—for example, writing or calling members of Congress to advise them how they should vote on a healthcare issue and why.
- **Lobbying:** National and state nursing organizations have lobbyists. Many of these organizations also have PACs that survey individuals running for office. They assess candidates' political platforms and endorse the political candidates they believe best represent their position.
- **Running for office:** Some nurses run for political office themselves, such as for a seat on the city council, for mayor, or for the state or national legislature.

The bottom line? It is important to be in tune with legislation that affects not only our practice as nurses but also reimbursement for healthcare services.

Accountable Care Organizations

An ACO is a group of doctors, hospitals, and other healthcare providers who voluntarily work together to give high-quality, coordinated care to a defined group of patients, most often Medicare patients. The goal is simple: improve outcomes, reduce unnecessary spending, and share in the savings if successful. Currently, reimbursement occurs in silos, with separate bills for acute care, rehab, home care, and so on. For example, suppose a patient receives a total hip replacement. That patient is initially seen in primary care. When a diagnosis is made, the patient is referred to an orthopedic specialist, who recommends a total hip replacement. The hip replacement is performed in the acute care setting, after which the patient is transferred to a rehab facility. The patient is then sent home, where they receive physical therapy. The patient receives separate bills from each of these settings. Figure 2.1 illustrates this model.

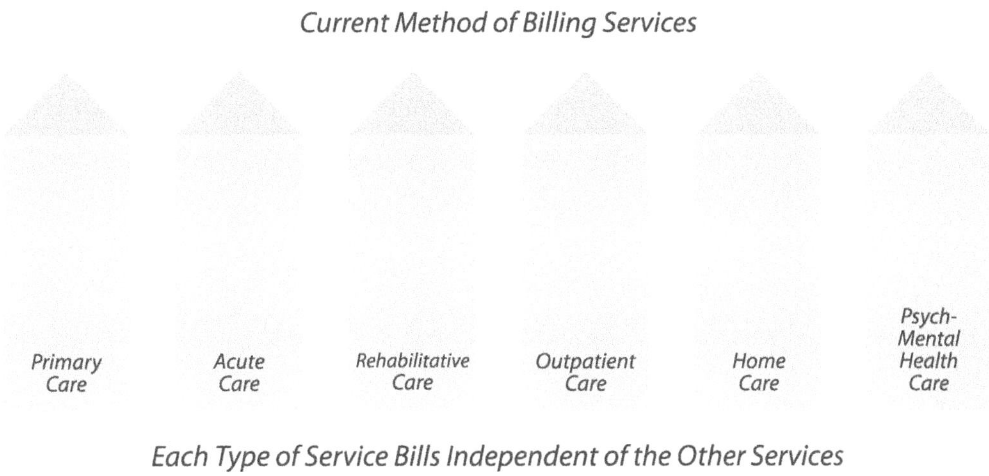

FIGURE 2.1
The current reimbursement model.

If one of the settings were to render poor-quality care, thus increasing the patient's length of stay, all these settings would suffer the consequences. Therefore, there is pressure on the provider rendering the poorer-quality care to improve; otherwise, the other providers could elect to partner with another provider that provides better quality (see Figure 2.2).

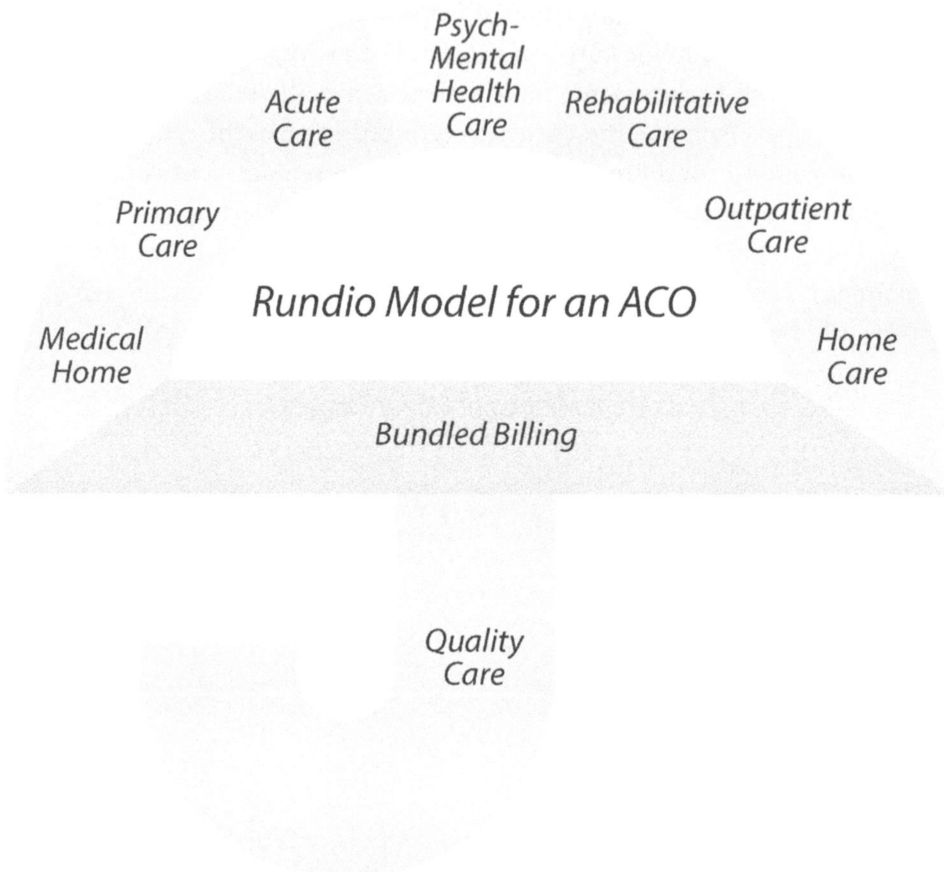

FIGURE 2.2
The ACO reimbursement model.

NOTE

In some ACO models, physicians become employees of the ACO, and their reimbursement level is correlated with the quality of care they provide. The better the quality, the higher the reimbursement to the provider.

New Rules

Another recent shift in social policy pertains to a push for more transparency for consumers regarding healthcare services and pricing. The CMS, in conjunction with the Department of Labor and the Department of the Treasury, established new rules under a 2019 executive order from the Trump administration. The new rules aimed to help ensure that all Americans know how much their healthcare will cost in advance, enabling them to make more informed decisions as healthcare consumers.

The new rules as staged with enforcement are as follows (Biniek et al., 2024; CMS.gov, 2020; Correa, 2025):

- Most private health plans, including group health plans and individual health insurance market plans, must disclose pricing and cost-sharing information.
- Group health plans and health insurance issuers in the individual and group markets must disclose how much they pay healthcare providers for specific services.
- Beginning January 1, 2022, plans had to make standardized and regularly updated data files publicly available to allow for new opportunities for research and innovation.
- Beginning January 1, 2023, health plans had to offer online shopping tools that enable consumers to see negotiated rates between their provider and their plan, as well as estimated out-of-pocket costs for 500 of the most commonly sought-after items and services.
- Beginning January 1, 2024, these shopping tools had to show costs for all remaining procedures, drugs, durable medical equipment, and any other item or service that consumers may need.
- Beginning January 1, 2026, plans had to publish a list of all items and services that required prior authorization and data on approval, denial, and turnaround rates.

Thanks to these new rules, more than 200 million Americans have gained access to real-time price information, promoting price transparency. The end result should be improvements in the healthcare market. However, this could be modified at any time. For example, in November 2025, CMS announced that it will no longer enforce regulations requiring health equity expertise, data reporting, or reasons for approving or denying care based on income, dual eligibility, and disability status for utilization management and prior authorization for Medicare Advantage plans (Correa, 2025). This is the second Trump administration move toward lessening oversight.

The Importance of Reimbursement: An Example

Budgeting in a hospital setting isn't so different from managing your personal checking and saving accounts. As an example, we all receive revenue for the work that we do in the form of a salary.

On the other side of the coin, we also have expenses. We have to pay for our mortgage or rent, car, electricity, food, clothing, and daily travel expenses (and other related expenses). If our expenses are greater than our income, we cannot pay all our bills. In other words, our expenses cannot exceed our income. All this is to say that we have money coming in and money going out on a daily, weekly, biweekly, monthly, and annual basis.

The same holds true for a hospital or healthcare system. If the hospital's reimbursements are lower than its expenditures, the hospital could go bankrupt. To break even, expenses will have to be reduced.

Managers need to know how to manipulate variables to produce the greatest cost benefit for their unit. Examples of such variables include staffing, staff mix, supplies, overtime, allocation of productive and nonproductive time, and other variables. This is not magic; it is a matter of using resources. Money comes in, and money goes out.

Problems Facing the Healthcare Delivery System

Today, the healthcare delivery system in the US faces a number of problems:

- **High costs:** The US spends far more per person on healthcare than any other developed country. Major drivers include hospital care, prescription drugs, and administrative costs. Due to decreasing revenue streams resulting from controlled and decreased reimbursement rates by managed care and from the federal government and state governments, it is becoming more and more difficult for healthcare organizations to make a profit or simply break even.
- **Access to care:** Millions remain uninsured or underinsured. In some rural communities, access to care has been limited due to hospital closures. Some individuals experience long wait times for primary care or behavioral health services that create delays in treatments, with worsening outcomes. There are approximately 26.7 million Americans with no healthcare insurance, and this estimate may be low given the high unemployment rates of the late 2000s (Tolbert et al., 2026) and the pandemic of 2020/2021. These individuals lack access to the system in the literal sense.
- **Workforce shortages:** Continued shortages in nursing and primary care create increased workload for those who remain, with lower morale and reduced access. Burnout of those who remain is an issue across all healthcare roles.
- **Health inequities:** It has become apparent that there are major disparities in healthcare outcomes by race, income, and geography. Chronic disease burden is much higher in underserved communities. Social determinants of health (housing, food access, transportation) play a large role in contributing to inequities.

- **Quality:** Although the US has some of the best technology available, our outcomes pale in comparison to those of other nations. Our healthcare delivery system focuses on intervention rather than prevention. Costly and invasive procedures and tests do not translate into improved outcomes.

The Effect of the COVID-19 Pandemic on Healthcare

Whoever thought that we would live through a pandemic? Well, in fact, the predictors were there. In 2009, the world faced an H1N1 influenza pandemic, also called the swine flu. Fortunately, the H1N1 virus proved to have much lower transmission rates than COVID-19 and a much lower death rate. Additionally, nurse executives and managers quickly demonstrated how they could control—and indeed almost completely eliminate—the H1N1 flu by limiting or eliminating visitation in most facilities and by making handwashing stations available in all areas of hospitals and other health facilities. (Many businesses, such as convenience stores and banks, followed suit.) The US averted a second pandemic in 2014—this one involving the Ebola virus. Due to excellent national control efforts, only a small number of people contracted this virus, which was eliminated in record time.

The eventual emergence of another pandemic—this one the COVID-19 virus, which emerged in the US in January of 2020—was not really a surprise. The world we live in has become a much smaller place thanks to the airline industry and the number of flights in and out of the US and around the world. This virus also proved difficult to contain because it is much more transmissible than previous viruses and affects all age groups. It is also much more deadly than H1N1 flu. And many individuals who contract COVID-19 also suffer from a post-viral syndrome.

Not surprisingly, the COVID-19 pandemic had a major effect on financial resources and operational management in healthcare. Still, interviews with chief financial officers and nurse executives made it very clear that patient and staff safety—*not* finances—were the top priorities. These individuals realized that if safety were not priority #1, the negative financial impact from failing to provide safe places would far exceed the costs of implementing safety protocols. Still, the effect of the pandemic was a decrease in reimbursement and increased costs that were not reimbursed.

Safety practices that had a negative financial impact on healthcare organizations during the COVID-19 pandemic include the following:

- Patients were unwilling to risk elective procedures such as colonoscopies and cancer screenings.
- Elective surgeries were stopped.
- The purchase of personal protective equipment became necessary.
- More negative pressure isolation rooms were needed.
- Patients needed to be tested for the presence of the virus.
- Staff needed to be tested. Indeed, some institutions tested all staff and patients once weekly—for example, nursing homes and assisted living facilities.
- Mask-wearing became the norm. In many facilities, all residents, clients, patients, and staff were required to wear masks at all times when in the company of others.
- Nurses with increased workloads and more difficult patients required crisis pay.
- Telehealth systems were implemented.
- Costs associated with environmental services and cleaning increased.

- Some organizations were forced to close for long periods of time—for example, dental practices (one of the highest risk categories).
- Normal supplies such as disinfectants, and other items such as toilet paper, became scarce and therefore more costly due to price gouging.

Needless to say, for management, decisions around where to allocate funds were quite difficult. With all these changes, and with increased testing, use of personal protective equipment, and wearing masks, one can readily see how the cost of operations at these facilities increased.

The COVID-19 pandemic caused other changes, too. Many state governors issued executive orders targeted toward halting the pandemic and caring for citizens. For example, in some states where advanced practice nurses must have collaborative agreements, governors issued executive orders granting these nurses temporary rights to full practice with no restrictions. Other executive orders sought to define what is considered an "essential service" and what is not. The main purpose of these executive orders was to keep citizens safe and to prevent deaths. However, these orders also had a devastating impact on the economy, only somewhat mitigated by federal efforts to provide financial relief to businesses, hospitals, and individuals.

> *"Control your own destiny or else someone else will."*
>
> *–Jack Welch*

Summary

This chapter covered:

- A political history of healthcare in the US
- An overview of healthcare reimbursement in the US
- Reimbursement for long-term care
- The role of social policy in healthcare reimbursement
- The importance of reimbursement

References

Biniek, J. F., Freed, M., & Neuman, T. (2024, April 10). *Gaps in Medicare Advantage data remain despite CMS actions to increase transparency.* Kaiser Family Foundation. https://www.kff.org/medicare/gaps-in-medicare-advantage-data-remain-despite-cms-actions-to-increase-transparency/

CMS.gov. (n.d.-a). *Your rights.* https://www.medicare.gov/basics/your-medicare-rights/your-rights

CMS.gov. (n.d.-b). *Nursing home care.* https://www.medicare.gov/coverage/nursing-home-care

CMS.gov. (n.d.-c). *Skilled nursing facility care.* https://www.medicare.gov/coverage/skilled-nursing-facility-care

CMS.gov. (2020, Oct. 29). *Transparency in coverage final rule fact sheet (CMS-9915-F).* https://www.cms.gov/newsroom/fact-sheets/transparency-coverage-final-rule-fact-sheet-cms-9915-f

CMS.gov. (2024, Sept. 10). *Grievances.* https://www.cms.gov/Medicare/Appeals-and-Grievances/MMCAG/Grievances

CMS.gov. (2026a, March 10). *Home health quality reporting requirements.* https://www.cms.gov/medicare/quality/home-health/home-health-quality-reporting-requirements

CMS.gov. (2026b, March 16). *Program of All-Inclusive Care for the Elderly (PACE).* https://www.cms.gov/medicare/medicaid-coordination/about/pace

Correa, C. (2025, Nov. 19). *CMS suspends new Medicare Advantage prior authorization transparency rules amid public concerns about care denials* [Blog]. Georgetown University Medicare Policy Initiative. https://medicare.chir.georgetown.edu/cms-suspends-new-medicare-advantage-prior-authorization-transparency-rules-amid-public-concerns-about-care-denials/

Justia. (n.d.). *Inland Steel Co. v. National Labor Relations Board, 109 F.2d 9 (7th Cir. 1940).* https://law.justia.com/cases/federal/appellate-courts/F2/109/9/1500899/

Medicare.gov. (n.d.). *What Part A covers.* https://www.medicare.gov/what-medicare-covers/what-part-a-covers

Medicare Rights Center. (2025, March 28). *The Part D donut hole*. Medicare Interactive. https://www.medicareinteractive.org/get-answers/medicare-prescription-drug-coverage-part-d/medicare-part-d-costs/the-part-d-donut-hole

Megellas, M. M. (2006). Medicare modernization: The new prescription drug benefit and redesigned Part B and Part C. *Baylor University Medical Center Proceedings, 19*(1), 21–23. https://doi.org/10.1080/08998280.2006.11928119

National Center for Drug Abuse Statistics. (2025). *Average cost of drug rehab.* https://drugabusestatistics.org/cost-of-rehab/

National Council on Aging. (2026, March 25). *The Medicare Part D donut hole: What you need to know.* https://www.ncoa.org/article/the-medicare-part-d-donut-hole-what-you-need-to-know/

O'Connor, M., & Davitt, J. K. (2012). The Outcome and Assessment Information Set (OASIS): A review of validity and reliability. *Home Health Care Service Quality, 31*(4), 267–301. https://doi.org/10.1080/01621424.2012.703908

Preskitt, J. T. (2008). Health care reimbursement: Clemens to Clinton. *Baylor University Medical Center Proceedings, 21*(1), 40–44. https://doi.org/10.1080/08998280.2008.11928358

Saunders, H., & Rudowitz, R. (2022, June 6). *Demographics and health insurance coverage of nonelderly adults with mental illness and substance use disorders in 2020*. Kaiser Family Foundation. https://www.kff.org/mental-health/demographics-and-health-insurance-coverage-of-nonelderly-adults-with-mental-illness-and-substance-use-disorders-in-2020/

Tolbert, J., Cervantes, S., Bell, C., & Damico, A. (2026, April 9). *Key facts about the uninsured population.* Kaiser Family Foundation. http://kff.org/uninsured/fact-sheet/key-facts-about-the-uninsured-population

Budget Types

Many new managers are unaware of the types of budgets that exist. Healthcare organizations use many types of budgets. These include:

- **Operating budget:** An *operating budget* is an overall plan for future operations, expressed in expenses and corresponding revenue. An operating budget is a formal quantification of an organization's goals and objectives—a road map for achieving its strategic mission. It's one of management's most widely used tools. You'll learn more about operating budgets in Chapter 5.
- **Capital budget:** A *capital budget* is for major capital, or investment, expenditures—the purchase of new equipment, the construction of new facilities, and so on. You'll learn more about capital budgets in Chapter 6.
- **Master budget:** A *master budget* is the budget for the entire organization.

- **Program budget:** A *program budget* is a budget for a specific program or operational unit within the organization.

In addition, the *cash budget* estimates future cash receipts and payments that are tabulated to demonstrate the forecasted cash balance.

NOTE

An organization's budget is intimately tied to its strategic mission—the main reason it exists—and to the goals and objectives it establishes to accomplish that mission. Organizations must be transparent—communicating the strategic vision and mission to all constituents within the organization—to create a budget.

Operating budgets and capital budgets are further broken down into *unit budgets*, so nurse managers can effectively develop, monitor, and manage their own budgets. Operating and capital budgets are the two budgets that nurse managers construct and monitor most often; therefore, these are discussed in more detail throughout this book.

> *"Budgeting has only one rule: Do not go over budget."*
>
> *–Leslie Tayne*

This chapter covers the three main components of the budget process, provides a glossary of key accounting terms, discusses responsibility center budgeting, and explains forms of budgets as well as historical budgets.

NOTE

Most budgets are constructed for a one-year time period, but many organizations now include periodic or rolling forecast updates into the process.

Assets, Liabilities, and Equity

There are three major accounting fundamentals that underpin budgets and financial statements (Jones et al., 2018):

- **Assets:** *Assets* are resources that are owned, usually stated as current assets, fixed assets, and noncurrent assets. Examples of current assets include cash and other assets that can be converted to cash within a one-year time period.
- **Liabilities:** Liabilities are the opposite of assets. A *liability* is an obligation that needs to be paid. Current liabilities are obligations due to be paid within a one-year time period. Examples include wages and taxes. Long-term liabilities are obligations or debts that are not due within a one-year time period.
- **Equity:** Equity is associated with assets and liabilities. *Equity* is the excess of assets over liabilities. These include resources invested by the owner. Some individuals refer to this as the *fund balance* or the *net worth.*

Equity can be increased or decreased. The way to increase equity is through investment by the owner and through the profits of an organization. The way to decrease equity is through the withdrawal of assets or cash or if there are losses from an unprofitable business.

The following equations help define assets and equity:

Assets = Liabilities + Equity

Equity = Assets – Liabilities

As an example, imagine a buyer wants to purchase a $350,000 home. The buyer puts down savings of $70,000 and obtains a mortgage for $280,000. You can apply the first equation as follows:

Assets = $350,000 Liability = $280,000 Equity = $70,000

A = L + E

($350,000 = $280,000 + $70,000)

Alternatively, you could apply the second equation in this way:

$$A - L = E$$

$$(\$350{,}000 - \$280{,}000 = \$70{,}000)$$

A Glossary of Basic Accounting Terms

Following are several basic accounting terms used in budgeting:

Accounting period: The period over which revenue and expenses are tracked. A *fiscal year* is a 12-month accounting period.

Accounts receivable: The funds that an organization is expecting to be paid. Accounts receivable are commonly received in anywhere from 60 to 90 days, but collection timelines vary widely by payer mix, denials, or contracting.

Bad debt: Revenue due to the organization that is not paid, either by the patient or the insurance company.

Balance sheet: A balance sheet reports an organization's assets as the sum of its liabilities plus its equity at a given point in time. Usually, the balance sheet is prepared at the end of a month or a year (see Table 3.1).

TABLE 3.1 BALANCE SHEET EXAMPLE

Current Assets		**Current Liabilities**	
Bank Account	$70,000.00	Accounts Payable	$10,000.00
Money Market	$100,000.00	Deferred Revenue (Dues 2020–2021)	$30,000.00
Bank Interest	$7,000.00	Total Deferred Revenue	$30,000.00
Total Bank Funds	**$177,000.00**	**Total Current Liabilities**	**$40,000.00**

Accounts Receivable	**$14,000.00**	**Net Assets**	
Property & Equipment	$22,000.00	Beginning Net Assets	$115,000.00
Accumulated Depreciation	$(11,000.00)	Restricted Chapters	$10,000.00
		Revenues Over (Under) Expenses	$50,000.00
P & E Net	**$11,000.00**	**Total Net Assets**	**$175,000.00**
Investments	$12,000.00		
Investments in & Advances to Affiliates	$1,000.00	Total Liabilities	$40,000.00
Total Assets	**$215,000.00**	**Total Liabilities & Net Assets**	**$215,000.00**

Break-even point: This is when revenue exactly equals total costs, including fixed costs and variable costs. The goal of any business is to have revenue exceed the break-even point.

Cash budget: An estimation of future cash receipts and payments that are tabulated to display the forecasted cash balance.

Days cash on hand: The amount of money an organization has available to it for immediate use in the event expenses exceed revenue. The amount varies substantially by organization type.

Real-World Example from Al Rundio: Cash on Hand

When I was a CNO, the hospital where I worked had approximately $70 million of board-designated funds, or cash on hand. One day, the CEO asked me, "If revenue were to suddenly cease, how long could the organization survive on the board-designated funds?" I quickly divided the board-designated funds ($70 million) by our monthly payroll ($4 million) and determined that we could sustain ourselves for

17.5 months. (In fact, we wouldn't have lasted even that long, because I based my estimate on payroll costs only, ignoring all the other costs we would need to pay to efficiently run our organization.)

Charity care: Uncompensated, free, or reduced-charge care provided by the organization. Some states fund care for individuals who do not have the ability to obtain health insurance (with varied rates), while others don't.

Direct cost: A cost that can be completely attributed to the production of a specific good or service. Examples of direct costs are materials, labor, and expenses related to the production of a product or within a specific work area. It is generally easier to control direct costs than indirect costs.

Expenses: Costs incurred by a business.

Fiscal year: A common accounting period. When a fiscal year begins and ends depends on the organization.

Understanding the Fiscal Year

Generally, budgets are designed for a one-year period. This is known as the *fiscal year.* The fiscal year will vary from organization to organization. In some states, the fiscal year begins on July 1 and ends on June 30. In other states, the fiscal year begins on January 1 and ends on December 31. Yet others have a fiscal year that begins on October 1 and ends on September 30. An organization's fiscal year might be dictated by the state in which the organization resides. It can also be chosen by the organization.

The fiscal year for the Centers for Medicare & Medicaid Services, the office that administers the federal Medicare and Medicaid programs, is October 1 to September 30. This can create problems for some organizations. For example, if Medicare enacts a reduction in reimbursement on October 1 but a hospital's fiscal year ends on June 30 of the following year, the hospital may run into financial difficulty.

Gross patient service revenue (GPSR): Charges for the provision of healthcare services to patients. The GPSR includes both inpatient and outpatient revenue. This is the "sticker price."

Indirect cost: A cost that is not directly associated with a single activity, event, or object. Such costs are usually aggregated into an overhead cost pool and allocated to various activities based on a perceived or actual linkage between the cost and the activity. Examples of indirect costs include management salaries and related benefits, quality assurance staff wages and related benefits, equipment maintenance, facility rental fees, and utilities. Other examples include depreciation and administrative expenses, which are more difficult to assign to a specific product. It is generally more difficult to control indirect costs than direct costs.

Net patient service revenue: The estimated net realizable amounts from patients, insurers, and others for services rendered. This includes contractual allowances—that is, discounts and estimated retroactive adjustments under reimbursement agreements with third-party payers, which translates to the negotiated payment price.

Profit: The amount of revenue that exceeds expenses. Also called *net income.*

$$\text{Profit} = \text{Revenue} - \text{Expenses}$$

Revenue: The amount of money received from customers for goods and services.

Real-World Example From Al Rundio: The Importance of Revenue

I cannot emphasize enough how important it is for an organization's revenue to exceed its expenses. Otherwise, it may fall behind paying its vendors. This can create a whole host of problems. I found this out the hard way when, while working as a staff nurse in an emergency department (ED), I noticed that the packaging of our Foley catheters had changed. Before, the catheter was packaged in a kit with KY gel and other necessary items. Now, however, I was forced to locate all these items separately. Upon further investigation, I discovered that the hospital had not been paying the vendor who supplied the kits, so the vendor had stopped sending the kits to the hospital. This forced the hospital to seek out other, less-expensive vendors, none of which offered a comparable kit.

Cash Basis Versus Accrual Basis

Revenues and expenses are generally measured on either a cash basis or an accrual basis. A *cash basis* approach, typically used by private practices, recognizes revenues when cash is received and when expenses are paid out. Advantages of a cash basis approach include:

- It enables you to see and compare how cash flows in and out of a business.
- It enables you to separate the cash one has available on hand from cash that has been billed but not yet received.

Disadvantages of a cash basis approach are:

- It does not recognize revenues that are earned but not yet received.

- It does not recognize liabilities to creditors.
- It does not recognize that expenses are resources that are used up; this becomes evident only when the money is paid out.

An *accrual basis* approach recognizes revenues when services have been performed or goods are sold. Similarly, expenses are recorded when the obligation is paid or the resource is used. An accrual basis approach offers a more accurate accounting of revenues and expenses. This approach is usually used by larger businesses, corporations, and hospitals and healthcare systems.

NOTE

One can easily see how a major event like a pandemic and all its associated costs could really sink an organization financially. This is discussed in more detail in Chapter 2.

Responsibility Center Budgeting

With traditional approaches to budgeting, operating units are generally held accountable for controlling direct costs, such as salaries and wages, materials and supplies, travel, and the acquisition and maintenance of equipment. This is because it is generally easier to control direct costs than indirect costs.

With responsibility center budgeting, all pertinent costs, and the revenue to support these costs, are assigned to various organizational units called *responsibility centers*. Put another way, responsibility center budgeting emphasizes specific costs in relation to well-defined areas of responsibility.

Responsibility Centers

A *responsibility center* is an organizational unit, area, or program. Another term for responsibility center is *operating unit.*

Some responsibility centers, such as pharmacies or laboratories, produce revenue. These types of responsibility centers are often referred to as *revenue centers.* Other responsibility centers don't produce revenue, such as units that focus on environmental services or administration. These types of centers are often referred to as *cost centers.* A department might consist of individual responsibility centers or a combination of several responsibility centers.

The idea behind responsibility center budgeting is to assign accountability to individuals who have the greatest potential to influence costs on a day-to-day basis. In nursing, this individual is usually the nurse manager for a nursing unit; however, this may vary from organization to organization.

NOTE

It is the reporting responsibility of these individuals to explain outcomes, regardless of the degree of their control or influence over results. So, the vice president of nursing might receive separate reports on the cost of operations for the medical-surgical nursing units, the critical care units, the ED, and operating rooms. Each individual unit will be held accountable for its respective area of responsibility.

Although it's true that direct costs are easier to control than indirect ones, that's not always the case. So, in addition to distinguishing between direct costs and indirect costs, responsibility center budgeting distinguishes between costs that are controllable and those that are not. Not every indirect cost is controllable at the responsibility center level. That being said, managers are often able to exercise considerable control over traditional indirect costs such as utilities and building maintenance.

NOTE

Costs such as depreciation, long-term lease arrangements, and other similar costs rarely qualify as controllable costs.

Responsibility centers have primary responsibility for the management of resources and costs, as well as the broader mission for which these resources and costs are budgeted and allocated. All sources of financial support—revenue or income—are attributed to the responsibility centers on some equitable and consistent basis. Costs associated with internal service units (that is, units that do not receive revenue or income from external sources, such as the environmental services department or the security department) are either charged to responsibility centers on a fee-for-service basis or are recovered from responsibility centers through some form of assessment.

After income/revenue and costs have been fully allocated to a responsibility center, there likely will be surpluses or deficits. While it's true that when budgets are prepared well, revenue should equal or even exceed costs, the reality is that this is very difficult to accomplish. Rarely does revenue equal costs. The goal, then, is to produce a surplus; at times, however, budget expenses exceed revenue, resulting in a deficit.

Deficits, or shortfalls, between total costs and revenues/income must be covered through some form of subvention. *Subvention* is a central allocation to ensure the continued operation of programs existing at the time the new allocation model is implemented. Some organizations create a subvention tax, or participation tax, for each responsibility center. The purpose of the tax is to make "whole" those responsibility centers that have a deficit shortfall. All responsibility centers participate in this tax—again, for the purpose of making all centers whole.

NOTE

Responsibility centers should be permitted to retain all or a major portion of their surpluses because this serves as an incentive to ensure that revenue and income exceed expenses.

One way to fund the subvention or participation tax is to take funds off the top—that is, to hold back some portion of the general funds to cover these costs. Another is to initiate a surcharge or assessment on the expenditure of the resources that have been fully allocated. The revenue collected through this levy could then be reallocated to the responsibility centers as subvention to provide a level playing field for those units faced with deficits and to seed additional activities that may have organization-wide benefits. A portion of the assessment could also be used to support internal service units.

NOTE

Responsibility center budgeting with a subvention tax is often used in universities—in particular, research-intensive universities. A portion of the subvention tax from each school or college within the university is applied to fund research activities across the university.

Forms of Budgets

Master budgets, operating budgets, capital budgets, and program budgets can take various forms. These include:

- **Zero-based budgets:** With a zero-based budget, expenses are justified from zero rather than rolled forward. The budget begins as a *tabula rasa*, or blank slate. The organization's finance department then estimates revenue and expenses based on an assessment of the community, national trends, market penetration of the organization, and so on. Zero-based budgets are completed for brand-new services or organizations and after major paradigm shifts. For example, suppose Medicare were to suddenly reimburse acute care hospital stays with a capitated reimbursement rate rather than a diagnosis-related groups rate. This would represent a paradigm shift in reimbursement practices, making it a good time for healthcare organizations to complete zero-based budgets.

- **Fixed budgets:** Organizations that are fiscally conservative generally adhere to a fixed budget. A fixed budget is prepared for the fiscal year and does not change for that entire year. However, many organizations start with a fixed annual budget baseline but do periodic forecasts or reforecasts to make adjustments as necessary.
- **Flexible budgets:** A flexible budget is completed for a fiscal year but is updated on a monthly or quarterly basis. For example, suppose patient volume has increased—and staffing along with it. In that case, a flexible budget would be adjusted accordingly to account for this increased volume.

The form used for a budget depends on the organization's philosophy. If the organization is fiscally conservative, a fixed budget is typically used. Some organizations are more flexible, in which case information in the budget might be updated quarterly rather than remaining static for a year. Zero-based budgets are performed periodically as a check and balance on a historical budget (discussed next), when a new service is implemented, or when a major paradigm shift in healthcare reimbursement has occurred.

NOTE

Completing a zero-based budget really forces organizations to justify every expense and reimbursement item.

Historical Budgets

Most institutions also generate a historical budget. This occurs on an annual basis. A *historical budget* reviews data from prior years, including the average daily census, hours per patient day, type of staffing, and so on. Based on this data, projections are made for the next fiscal year. The data in historical budgets can also be used as baseline data.

Data from recent history is vital to the development of historical budgets. Usually, the first eight months of operation are reviewed. A budget for the following year is then developed. Responsibility center/unit-based managers review the proposed budgets and make recommendations and adjustments. Then, this budget is updated with information from months 9 and 10 of the current fiscal year.

"An investment in knowledge pays the best interest."

–Benjamin Franklin

TIP

You should complete a zero-based budget as a check and balance on an organization's historical budget. This forces each expense item, as well as each revenue item, to be justified. Zero-based budgets do not rely on historical data.

Summary

This chapter covered:

- Assets, liabilities, and equity
- A glossary of basic accounting terms
- Responsibility center budgeting
- Forms of budgets

- Historical budgets
- Operating budgets versus capital budgets
- Strategic vision and mission
- Cash basis of accounting

Reference

Jones, C. B., Finkler, S. A., Kovner, C. T., & Mose, J. N. (2018). *Financial management for nurse managers and executives* (5th ed.). W. B. Saunders.

CHAPTER 4

Budget Development

In most organizations, nurse managers set goals and design the budget—usually in collaboration with the finance department—for their own responsibility center or nursing unit. After the budget has been developed and updated, it is submitted for approval to administration and ultimately to the board of directors. After the budget is approved and the fiscal year begins, the organization must deliver the planned services and programs.

The budgeting process is ongoing and dynamic and should provide feedback. This is essential in managing the budget. The budget-development workflow involves these steps:

1. Collecting relevant data
2. Planning services
3. Planning activities
4. Implementing the plan
5. Monitoring the budget
6. Taking corrective measures when necessary

> *"Be aware of little expenses. A small leak can sink a great ship."*
> *–Benjamin Franklin*

NOTE

Spreadsheets, typically in Microsoft Excel, are used to calculate all budget components at the unit level.

Step 1: Collecting Relevant Data

A critical task in creating a budget is collecting relevant data. The finance department ultimately collects this data but does so in collaboration with the nurse manager to create a functional budget. This includes:

- **Services offered:** This data is collected by the nurse manager, who has the most insight into services currently on offer and those that will be offered in the future. For example, a nurse manager might plan to increase bed capacity in an underused nursing unit in response to an increase in the census in the past year and the knowledge that an additional surgeon will be coming on staff, which will increase volume even more.
- **Patient mix/case mix:** This pertains to the complexity of care. Generally, the more complex the case, the higher the reimbursement, depending on payer methodology (DRG weights, outliers, negotiated rates, quality adjustments, denials, etc.). The finance department of every hospital and skilled nursing facility calculates an overall case-mix index to provide a benchmark, but reimbursement may be influenced by contract and quality/denial dynamics. See example below in acuity index.
- **Payer mix:** This number, also calculated by the finance department, reflects patient demographics. For example, suppose the payer mix indicates that 50% of the patients of a healthcare facility are below the age of 65 and have commercial insurance. Generally, for such patients, the length of stay (LOS) is shorter and reimbursement is

higher than for Medicare patients. Now suppose the payer mix indicates that 70% of a facility's patients are over 65 and that their primary insurance is Medicare. For these patients, the length of stay will typically be longer and reimbursement lower than for patients with commercial insurance. However, in many markets, reimbursement/LOS patterns vary widely by contract terms, site-of-care shifts, Medicare Advantage plans, bundled/value-based arrangements, and population differences. Therefore, this calculation provides an input for performance analysis, not a deterministic predictor of reimbursement.

- **Acuity index:** This is a numeric calculation that considers the acuity of each patient in a given nursing unit to predict the level of staffing required. It used to be that the nurse manager or charge nurse on each shift assessed each patient in the unit and assigned a numeric acuity level to each one to calculate the acuity index. Because these were subjective assessments, however, the index could be inaccurate, typically predicting the need for huge increases in staffing that the organization could not afford. Today, most facilities use hybrid models combining acuity, census, benchmarks, and clinical judgment to provide decision support for this calculation.

NOTE

Some facilities do not use acuity systems. Instead, predictions for average, minimum, and maximum staffing requirements are based on census information, the type of nursing unit, and data from organizations that report nursing hours per patient day, for example, a state's hospital association. This varies by organization, however; some utilize robust tools while others may still use the older system of census and benchmarks. Every day, new changes arise in the technology arena. Some organizations are utilizing computerized acuity systems that will impact this process in the near future.

In addition, the following data should be gathered:

- Hours provided per patient day or visit
- Standards of care
- Plans for changes in services provided
- Plans for changes in resource utilization

All this information can be gleaned from these data sources:

- **Historical information:** This is composed of the prior years' history of operational performance found in budget reports. Information such as patient days, average length of stay, nursing hours per patient day, staff overtime, and so on are reviewed from prior years to make budget projections for the upcoming year.
- **Statistical reports/prior year reports:** Statistical reports record one year of operations in an organization. After the year is up, a statistical report becomes a prior year report—part of the organization's history. In organizations that do historical budgeting, the finance department and the nurse manager refer to prior year reports when creating the budget for the next fiscal year.
- **Industry trends:** An example of an industry trend is a change in technology. For example, some orthopedic total hip replacements now take an anterior approach, with the patient discharged the next day rather than enduring a three-day hospital stay. This affects reimbursement. Another example is the use of percutaneous cardiac interventions rather than coronary bypass surgeries in myocardial infarction patients. Other industry trends could relate to things happening in politics, such as decreasing reimbursement in the Medicare or Medicaid programs.
- **Organizational goals and objectives:** These are developed by the top administration and are generally communicated to staff through department directors and administrators. Nurse managers formulate

their own goals and objectives, which must be aligned with the overall organizational goals and objectives.

Real-Life Example From Al Rundio: Historical Budgets

From my experience speaking around the country, I've learned that most facilities see historical budgeting as a vital component of planning the next fiscal year's budget. When I was a chief nursing officer (CNO), the finance department always provided me with useful historical information—usually from the previous four or five years—whenever I was planning the next year's budget. Reviewing data from previous years, I could quickly identify patterns and trends—for example, whether the average patient length of stay or admissions were increasing, decreasing, or remaining level, and whether there had been practice changes that drive patient length of stay (e.g., when total hip replacements changed from an average length of stay of 15 days to one day). One of the data elements that I really homed in on was the nursing hours of care per patient day.

It is often sensible to review historical data from a shorter time period when major paradigm shifts in healthcare reimbursement occur. For example, in New Jersey, all private insurance companies used to reimburse for acute inpatient hospital care using a DRG system. Then in 1992, the governor deregulated the healthcare insurance reimbursement industry in our state. This meant that from 1992 on, insurance companies negotiated rates individually with each hospital or hospital system. It also cleared the way for managed care. Afterward, anyone looking at historical data for New Jersey could clearly see a difference in average length of stay, admissions, and nursing hours per patient day. When we prepared budgets for 1993 and 1994, information prior to 1992 was suddenly rather outdated. It just did not make sense to track back too many years until the new system stabilized.

NOTE

Nurses must be attuned to what the federal government does with federal insurance programs as well as what their state government does with Medicaid, charity care, and other state-managed programs.

Understanding the Chart of Accounts

During the budget-creation process, the finance department will create a *chart of accounts*. This is a list of income (revenue), expense (what the business spends), liability (what the business owes), and asset (what the business owns) accounts used in maintaining their books in a general ledger.

The chart of accounts is set up by the finance department at the start of the business. Reference numbers are used to help classify the accounts by type. For example, in a hospital, each nursing unit will have a reference number. The chart organizes and tracks all business activities. Reports can then be easily generated in a logical sequence to track the financial history and progress of the business.

The chart of accounts does the following:

- It provides a format for the financial structure of the budget so that all expenses and revenues can be tracked and recorded.
- It structures the recording and reporting of activities (revenue and expense).
- It organizes the information.
- It identifies the various areas of responsibility and the types of transactions that occur in each.

You can think of a chart of accounts as being like a household budget. In a household budget, which many people organize in columns in a table format, they list revenue—that is, primary income from a job, consulting, or sale. Then they list expense items—for example, mortgage, car payment, utilities, credit card bills, tuition, and so on. Each column includes total amounts—for example, total income and total expenses.

There are some differences between a chart of accounts and a household budget. Al Rundio gives the following example: "I recently paid off the mortgage for my house, so I no longer need to list the mortgage amount as an expense. However, even though my home is an asset, I don't list it as such in my household budget. In contrast, a chart of accounts for a business *would* list the value of any fully owned assets—for example, physical plants. The chart of accounts would also list any liabilities."

Most nurse managers neither see nor prepare charts of accounts. Doing so is an accounting function of the finance department. However, it is important for nurse managers to know these exist and what they are for.

Step 2: Planning Services

The nursing department is generally aware of what types of services will be rendered in the next fiscal year. However, although the finance department may be aware of large projects, it might not be cognizant of every type of service that will be rendered.

If you are planning a new service for the next fiscal budget, this must be communicated to the finance department. For example, suppose a nurse manager in an emergency department (ED) is planning to launch a fast-track service to accommodate minor emergencies more efficiently. Because this new service will require additional staffing, the budget will have to be formulated with it in mind. That is, all associated costs, as well as projected volume and revenue, will need to be accounted for in the budget. It's crucial that the finance department be aware of this.

It is imperative that nurse executives work effectively with the individuals in their organization who control the purse strings. This is why you should always cultivate an ongoing relationship with the finance department wherever you work. Meet frequently with the budget manager, who also meets with the managers on a routine basis. Often, during budget-preparation time, the budget manager will meet individually with unit managers to plan the next fiscal year's budget. The purpose of all these meetings is to review current finance reports and to communicate current and future activities and planning. During my tenure as CNO, our chief executive officer (CEO) would meet with me and each department director during the budget prep time to understand their needs and communicate the organizational plans. This enabled us to construct a budget that was understood by all staff.

There will almost always be budget surprises during a fiscal year. These, too, must be communicated to finance.

Real-World Example from Al Rundio: Budget Surprises

Back when laparoscopic surgery was in its infancy, some of our medical staff trained on the procedure and decided they wanted to implement it mid–budget year. This would involve some costs—for example, the purchase of new equipment for the operating room. These costs weren't huge, but they were unplanned. The CNO communicated this to the finance department, the chief financial officer (CFO), and the CEO. She explained that equipping ourselves to perform these surgeries would increase revenue in the long run and that we would lose market share if we did not do it now. We then as a united group sold this to the board of directors, who approved the purchase of the equipment for the implementation of this new procedure.

With mid–budget year requests, it's critical to really analyze what is being requested. Ask yourself these questions:

- Can it wait until the next fiscal year?
- Will we lose market share if we delay purchase or implementation?
- What are the overall costs?
- Do the costs outweigh the benefits?
- Will revenue increase?

Step 3: Planning Activities

An example of an activity is a treatment offered by a department. New activities must be accounted for in the budget. Consider this older but simple example: When tissue plasminogen activator (TPA) became available to treat myocardial infarction patients in EDs, nurse managers were aware of this, but individuals in the finance department likely were not. This was a problem because TPA costs approximately $2,000 per treatment. So, if the ED treated 2,000 myocardial infarction patients every year, and 75% of these patients could receive TPA, the cost would be upwards of $3 million. If the nurse manager failed to make the finance department aware of this new treatment and the associated costs, there would be a significant negative budget variance. Finance would also need to see if insurance would reimburse this new treatment. You can see why the nurse manager is critical to planning activities for the budget!

Defending Your Proposals

Often, creating a budget involves defending what you have proposed. This goes for nurse managers, too. Defending what you are proposing is a give-and-take process, based on the available resources of the organization.

One of the more challenging proposals to justify is a new nursing position or role. Take the role of clinical nurse specialist on a nursing unit. There is no doubt that a good clinical nurse specialist improves care and mentors and motivates nursing staff to excel. Adding a new clinical nurse specialist position to the budget, however, has to be justified. Providing concrete outcome measurement data from the clinical specialists in the role can enable the nurse manager to get approval on these positions. Consider the impact of this role. When I was adding clinical nurse specialist positions to my unit, I utilized outcome measures like reduced ventilator-acquired pneumonia, decreased central line bloodstream infections, lowered hospital-acquired pressure injuries, and reduced staff turnover as some metrics for justification.

In any case, it's generally true that when estimating the staffing and dollars needed to deliver care, the nursing department's figure will be higher than the finance group's. So, nursing and finance must come to agreement on the budget before presenting it to administration. Having these two departments in agreement becomes an item of defense if the CEO does not approve the budget as submitted.

Speaking of the CEO, they will most likely question certain budgeted items. The item questioned most often is the care hours provided per patient day because these hours convert to staffed hours. Usually, nursing attempts to increase the hours. Care hours provided should be aligned with the complexity of the cases and the acuity system used (if any).

During the COVID-19 pandemic, our CEO could not understand the need for additional staff related to proning. She envisioned proning as "flipping the patient over." Well, sometimes a good visual is the best example. We took a stroll over to the ICU and observed the team in the action of proning. This was eye-opening for our CEO. She now understood the time and resources needed and the complexity of proning. By understanding this, we were able to partner to ensure our staff and patients had the best care we could provide.

Understanding the complexity of your practice details is important. Your best bet is to prepare for and anticipate all questions and to back up your answers with data. For example, if you predict more care hours due to an increased census, answer the following questions to gather the data needed to justify your request:

- How has the census increased during the past year?
- What percent of occupancy does your unit have and for how long?
- How will this trend continue into the foreseeable future?
- What is unique about this patient population?

The finance department can help you with this.

Step 4: Implementing the Plan

After upper-level administration and the board of directors approve the budget plan, the nurse manager implements it. Implementing the plan means providing the services. It's what occurs on a day-to-day basis with the provision of care to patients. Often, the process of implementing the budget plan will be similar from year to year. Sometimes, however, it might entail the enactment of new services or treatments.

NOTE

During the implementation process, budgeted expenses and revenue are compared to actual expenses and revenue.

Step 5: Monitoring the Budget

The budget must be monitored. Monitoring the budget involves the following:

- Routinely generating accurate financial reports
- Using these financial reports to compare actual revenue and expenses to budgeted revenue and expenses and identify variances
- Conducting variance analysis to examine variances in cost, efficiency, and volume

NOTE

Chapter 8 discusses various types of budget reports.

Who does what may vary from organization to organization. For example, the finance department usually generates reports, while the nurse manager typically identifies variances and conducts variance analysis. However, this might not always be the case.

Variance analysis is especially critical whenever there is a deficit—that is, when actual expenses exceed budgeted expenses or actual revenue is less than budgeted revenue. This is so that the nurse manager can determine exactly what is causing the problem. Armed with this knowledge, the nurse manager can take corrective action in the next budget cycle. It is important to understand that variances are often smoothed out across the budget cycle. For example, if there is a large purchase that hits one month, it will cause a large variance in that month. Some organizations spread this over the cycle, while others account for it in the single month. Knowing how your organization manages this, and being able to justify it, is essential.

Step 6: Taking Corrective Measures When Necessary

Goals set forth in the budget may need to be modified depending on performance. A change in the types and levels of services and the resources used may also be required. To illustrate, recall the TPA example from earlier in this chapter. Suppose that everything is going well with the administration of TPA and that the first quarter budget report is right on target. Now suppose that new evidence emerges during the second quarter that demonstrates that patients with an acute myocardial infarction should be treated promptly in a cath lab so that percutaneous cardiac interventions can be performed—for example, an angioplasty with stent placement. This evidence drives the decision to immediately begin triaging patients right to the cardiac cath lab instead of administering TPA in the ED. So, because fewer patients will receive TPA in the ED, that department will need to reduce its projected costs and revenue accordingly. Similarly, because the cath lab will see *more* patients, it will need to adjust its budget to account for more staffing and on-call shifts.

Management's Role in Budgeting

In terms of budgeting, management responsibilities are broken down as follows:

- **Department head:** Each department head or nurse manager is responsible for confirming the detailed operating expense budget for their department (cost center), consistent with organizational goals and objectives.
- **Director of budget:** The director of budget ensures that all budget forms are properly prepared and that data is accumulated within the specified timetable.

- **Vice presidents:** Vice presidents are responsible for the establishment of the basic annual budget formulation parameters. They assimilate departmental budgets into an organizational master budget consistent with organizational goals and objectives.
- **President/CEO:** The president or CEO has overall responsibility for the formulation and execution of the organization's budget. The president ensures consistency between the budget and divisional goals and objectives.
- **Finance committee and board of trustees:** These bodies are responsible for the review and approval of the completed operating budget.

In a healthcare setting, department heads and nurse managers are involved with some of the most critical functions in budgetary planning and the control process. They serve as the link between the plans of administration and the performance of the institution's workforce. If they fail to achieve the objectives and goals of the budget, the desired results will not be achieved.

Spotting a Dysfunctional Budget

Managers consider a budget to be dysfunctional when it is seen to be:

- **Rigid:** Some fiscal departments are very conservative. So, when the budget is created for the next year, it is more or less set in stone, or rigid. Even if variances are identified and explained, the budget will not change.
- **Externally imposed:** In some organizations, the budget is externally imposed by a higher administrative person—for example, a director of nursing. In one scenario, this person completes the budget with the finance budget manager and simply hands it down to nurse managers without their input. In another

scenario, the nurse manager has an opportunity to offer input—for example, calling for more staffing—but higher administration determines that the request is not feasible. The nurse manager must then manage within the confines of the budget provided.

- **Interfering with interdepartmental/intradepartmental cooperation and communication:** Departmental cooperation and communication can suffer when one department receives more in the budget than another department. For example, suppose the nurse manager puts in a request in the capital budget for a new automatic blood pressure machine, but it is denied. Now suppose the radiology department puts in a request for a new CT scanner, and it is approved. The CT scanner is in the million-dollar range. The automatic blood pressure machine is in the thousand-dollar range. The nurse manager's working relationship with the radiology director suffers because of this.
- **A tool for which managers are held accountable but do not have the authority to control:** Often, the nurse manager is held accountable for the budget but is not given the authority to control it. For example, one manager never saw the budget or the budget reports. Still, two years into the job, that manager was reprimanded for using too much overtime. Essentially, the manager was held accountable for the overtime, but because she had no access to the necessary reports, she had no authority to really manage it!

Inventory Management

In a healthcare setting, *inventory management* involves overseeing and controlling the ordering, storage, and use of supplies needed for the provision of care. A healthcare organization's inventory is one of its major assets.

Inventory is an investment that is tied up until the item is used. It also costs money to store, track, and insure inventory. Mismanagement of inventories can create significant financial problems for a healthcare entity, resulting in inventory excess or an inventory shortage.

NOTE

Hospitals and other healthcare organizations require that a lot of inventory be kept on hand for daily use. The amount kept available is based on prior history and projected volumes for an upcoming fiscal cycle.

Successful inventory management involves creating a purchasing plan that ensures that items are available when they are needed—but that neither too much nor too little is purchased—and keeping track of existing inventory and its use. Two common inventory-management methods are as follows:

- **Just-in-time ordering:** With this method, companies plan to receive items as they are needed rather than maintaining high inventory levels. Waiting to order a very expensive and rarely used surgical device until a patient schedules a procedure that requires it is an example of just-in-time ordering.
- **Materials requiring planning:** With this method, companies schedule material deliveries based on projected forecasts.

Inventory management also includes rotating stock, checking stock for outdated or near-outdated supplies, and making certain that supplies are on hand when needed.

One area in a hospital with particularly high inventory costs is the operating room. In most operating rooms, there is a procedure or preference card for each type of surgical procedure. This card lists all the inventory items required for a procedure. Hospitals often design their informatics system so that when a nurse pulls the inventory for a procedure (based on the procedure/preference card), the system automatically bills the patient's account and orders replacement inventory. This ensures that the correct amount of inventory is on hand and that the correct party is billed for the inventory. It also controls costs because excessive inventory is not maintained; items are replaced only when they are used.

The Importance of Paying Vendors

One Friday afternoon, knowing that Friday evenings often brought numerous trauma patients to the facility, the nurse manager at a busy inner-city ED checked the supply room for lactated Ringer's solution. After an extensive search, the nurse manager concluded that there were no bags of lactated Ringer's solution on the shelf.

The nurse manager called the central processing department that stocked supplies to ask why there was no lactated Ringer's solution. The answer was that they had run out of it. Upon further questioning, the nurse manager learned that the hospital was experiencing financial difficulty and had not been paying its vendors. The vendor that supplied the lactated Ringer's solution would not send more bags of it until payment was received.

Healthcare organizations that fail to pay vendors for inventory place the organization in jeopardy, as eventually the vendor will stop providing supplies. Vendor disputes like these *must* be addressed before a situation like this one unfolds. A well-functioning purchasing department would never allow such an event to occur. An astute purchasing manager stays on top of these issues so that the supply chain is not impacted. Vendors must be paid in a timely manner—especially for critical supplies. Imagine what would happen if the company that supplied the hospital's oxygen was not paid, and no oxygen was delivered!

The key is to negotiate reasonable charges. This can be done in several ways. One way is to explore how many companies make or distribute a particular item and obtain price quotes from all of them. Another is to work with multiple hospitals in a network to obtain a lower group price.

In this example, the ED in question was part of a two-hospital system, and fortunately, the other hospital had extra lactated Ringer's solution on hand to share. In an emergency, however, other crystalloid solutions, such as normal saline solution, could have been used.

Contingency Management

Contingency management is a management approach that involves identifying potential threats and vulnerabilities and implementing countermeasures to limit their impact should they occur (Nordmeyer, n.d.). The COVID-19 pandemic has clearly demonstrated the importance of contingency management with regard to the supply chain.

As CNO during this time, I took contingency management very seriously from the beginning of the pandemic. We assembled key individuals to form an oversight committee, which met daily, and communicated during our daily safety huddle. We had daily inventory checks and locked PPE supplies in a special room we called the Vault. All supplies were signed out. We worked with the state's department of health, which updated incident rates daily. As a result, we had enough PPE, patient care equipment (such as ventilators, ED beds, and ICU beds), and so on, available at all times. The partnering of senior leadership, department directors and managers, and frontline staff enabled this to be successful.

This committee also paid close attention to the vaccine trials. Four months before the FDA approved the Pfizer vaccine, the committee predicted that this would likely be the first vaccine approved and purchased the subzero refrigerators needed to store it. Again, this was *four months* before vaccine approval!

This story demonstrates what predictive analytics and a proactive organization can accomplish.

Interview With a Chief Nursing Officer

I interviewed a well-respected and seasoned chief nursing officer who is part of a large, quaternary healthcare system.

Q. ***What is the nursing management structure in your organization?***

A. CNO → senior director or director → nurse manager → assistant nurse manager → charge nurse

Q. ***Does your organization use an acuity system to determine nurse staffing levels?***

A. No. However, the staffing models allow for some flexibility based on patient acuity. For example, in the ICU there can be 1:1 or 1:2 assignments based on the patient's acuity on that day.

Q. ***How is the nursing budget developed?***

A. Prior to the budget packages being sent out, volume meetings are held by service line with the directors, VPs, C-suite executives, and so on to look at healthcare trends in the region—hospital closures, anticipated volumes based on new surgeons, and more. Packages for the operational budgets are then sent to the department head from finance with a return date to make revisions and negotiate potential changes. Meetings are then scheduled with finance, department heads, and the CNO to finalize.

Q. ***What percent of staff are registered nurses versus other types of staff?***

A. 60% RNs vs. ancillary support staff. We do not utilize LPNs.

Q. ***How do you determine nursing hours of care per patient day?***

A. We belong to Vizient and utilize this database to help determine the appropriate HPPD based on like organizations/departments. We benchmark at the 60th percentile when determining the HPPD.

Q. ***What effect has the COVID-19 pandemic had on the organization?***

A. During COVID and immediately after we did have some nurse turnover. Some went into travel positions because of the high rates being given, and some just left the profession. The workforce has stabilized, and turnover is back to normal levels.

One thing that has changed dramatically since COVID is the incidents of workplace violence against healthcare workers, exposing them to unprecedented levels of aggression—incidents of verbal abuse, threats, and physical assaults.

Summary

This chapter discussed:

- The six steps of the budget-development workflow
- Management's role in budgeting
- Inventory management

Reference

Nordmeyer, B. (n.d.). What is contingency management in a business? *Chron.* https://smallbusiness.chron.com/contingency-management-business-23285.html

Operating Budgets

As mentioned in Chapter 3, the *operating budget* is the overall plan for future operations, expressed in expense funds and corresponding revenue funds. The operating budget attempts to consider all revenues and expenses of an organization. Of course, the goal is to have revenues exceed expenses. The creation of the operating budget should be a joint effort by the administration and management teams.

The operating budget is one of management's most widely used tools for financial planning and controlling the organization. Although the operating budget is not in itself a management tool, it becomes one through management action. If a manager does not take action to correct budget performance—which, let's face it, some never do—then the operating budget is useless.

> *"A budget is a tool for planning, quantifying the plans, and controlling the costs."*
>
> *–Henry Finkler*

NOTE

Management action is critical to managing the operating budget.

Analyzing Budget Differences

If you detect a budget difference—for example, you determine that expenses have gone up—you must analyze the variance to identify its root cause. For example, an organization uses special kits when IV lines are started. The kit costs the organization $3. The organization charges $5 to insert the line. One would think that the net revenue is $2. However, you must consider the labor costs involved, and then you will have a better estimate of the net revenue.

Now imagine that expenses went up during the next monthly budget period. To analyze the root cause of the budget difference, you might ask these questions:

- Did volume increase?
- Did the cost of the IV start kits increase?
  - Which component of the kit increased in price?
  - Did the supplier change?
- Was there a significant increase in labor costs?
- Are there newer staff that may be using additional kits when starting IV lines?
- Does a new kit need to be opened every time, or are there components available separately?

An increase in expenses isn't always bad. If more IV lines are started than anticipated, that is easily explained in the variance, but if volumes are the same, there is another cause that must be identified.

The operating budget projects anticipated activities and the resources required to support the planned activity. It is a projection of revenues and expenses for a given time period (usually one year). It has a framework within the financial structure and reporting mechanisms of the organization.

Specifically, the operating budget is based on the following:

- Anticipated levels of output, including:
    - The number of admissions
    - The number of patient days
    - Departmental activity
    - New services/programs
- Predetermined hospital goals and objectives
- Agreement with the strategic/long-range plan

Key Metrics in the Operating Budget

When creating the operating budget, a key metric for managers is the workload for the next year. *Workload* is the amount of work performed by a unit. It is often measured in units of service, which are used to determine revenues and resource requirements.

To calculate all this, you need some key statistics concerning current activity. These include:

- **Census:** The number of beds occupied every day (usually at midnight).
- **Occupancy rate:** The percentage of the total number of beds filled.
- **Average daily census (ADC):** The number of patient days on average over a specific period of time. (To obtain this statistic, divide the number of patient days by the number of days in the specific time period.)

- **Average length of stay:** The average number of days that one is an inpatient. (To obtain this statistic, divide the number of inpatient days by the total number of patients.)

Of course, another critical metric is revenue. Once upon a time, nurse managers were not privy to this information. The thinking in the finance department was that if nurse managers were not made aware of the revenue, they would not know whether the organization was making money or losing money. As a result, the finance department could always push nurse managers to control or cut expenses. Today, the opposite is true. Now, nurse managers in the vast majority of organizations *do* see the revenue side of the equation. Indeed, nurse managers are urged to consider their responsibility center or unit as their own mini business center, each with its own characteristics and needs, with the goal of maximizing profits.

NOTE

For individual responsibility/cost centers, the revenue listed on the financial report generally acknowledges variation from budget. It is important for managers to understand exactly what is included in the revenue so they are able to submit accurate variance reports.

Sources of revenue include:

- Payment for patient services, which is broken down into two categories:
    - **Gross patient service revenue (GPSR):** Gross charges at established rates for the provision of health services to patients. This includes both inpatient and outpatient services. Gross-to-net revenue is driven by payer contracts and reimbursement, while managers most often influence volume, documentation quality, and avoidable costs per case.

  - **Net patient service revenue (NPSR):** The estimated net revenue that the organization actually sees. This might deviate from GPSR if, for example, an insurance company denies reimbursement for a procedure or service, and the patient is not able to cover the difference. It might also differ due to *contractual allowances*, which are negotiated discounts given by the organization to insurance companies and other third-party payers. In this case, patients cannot be billed the difference for such circumstances.
- Payment for inpatient treatment and care
- Payment for outpatient treatment and care

Other sources of revenue include money earned from the cafeteria, gift shop, parking fees, and investment income.

Revenue is based on the price, or charge, set for specific services. However, as mentioned, almost no one pays full price. For example:

- Medicare pays a fixed amount per inpatient, based on the discharge diagnosis.
- Medicaid generally pays less than the stated charges, with the amount varying from state to state.
- Third-party payers, or insurance companies, pay a negotiated discounted rate—the contractual allowance.
- Charity care may or may not cover all or part of a service based on certain criteria—for example, financial need, geographic region, and other indicators.

These factors can increase the difference between an organization's GPSR and its NPSR. Another factor that may increase this difference is bad debt. As noted in Chapter 2, bad debt accrues when healthcare facilities receive no reimbursement for care given, either because an insurance provider denies payment or a patient cannot pay.

It follows, then, that NPSR, or net revenue, is the key metric. To obtain the net revenue, use the simple formula:

Gross Revenue – Deductions from Revenue = Net Revenue

The Red and the Black

The difference between the amount collected from payers, patients, and other sources and the amount hospitals spend to provide care is called the *operating margin*. When revenue exceeds expenses (the goal), an organization is said to have a *black* bottom line. A *red* bottom line is when expenses exceed revenue, and the organization has lost money.

Understanding Expenses

For individual responsibility/cost centers, expenses listed on financial reports are generally direct expenses—that is, expenses tied to activity in that responsibility/cost center. There are two main types of direct expenses:

- **Direct patient care costs:** Examples of these include staff nurse salaries, dressing supplies, IV fluids, and so on.
- **Indirect patient care costs:** These support the overall operation of the area. Examples include seminars, conferences, continuing education hours, office supplies, and so on. Indirect patient care costs also include costs shared by all departments, such as lighting, heating, and administrative and other personnel costs.

Expenses are also sorted into *employment costs* (also called *salary-related expenses*) and *non-salary expenses*. Employment costs are categorized as follows:

- **Type of employee:** Types might include doctor, RN, patient care tech, pharmacist, pharmacy tech, and so on.

- **Type of hours paid:** Examples include regular time, overtime, vacation hours, holiday hours, sick hours, and so on.
- **Type of differential paid:** Types include shift differential, on-call pay, and so on.
- **Benefits paid:** Examples include health insurance, FICA, matching 401K, gain sharing, and so on.

Then there are non-salary expenses. Examples of these include:

- Office supplies
- Major movable equipment
- Professional journal subscriptions
- Instruments
- General patient care supplies

In addition to these are expenses incurred by a department and charged to the patient. These include:

- Telephone calls
- Internet/TV connection
- Stock medications
- Central supplies
- Linen supplies

The percentage difference between expenses and revenue is called the *profit margin*. In today's economic climate, it is becoming more difficult for healthcare organizations to have a positive profit margin.

As you learned in Chapter 3, the point at which revenue covers expenses is called the *break-even point*. The goal of any business is to have revenue exceed the break-even point. The break-even point is usually represented on a graph with two diagonal lines. In this graph, one line represents revenue and the other represents expenses; the break-even point is where both lines intersect (see Figure 5.1).

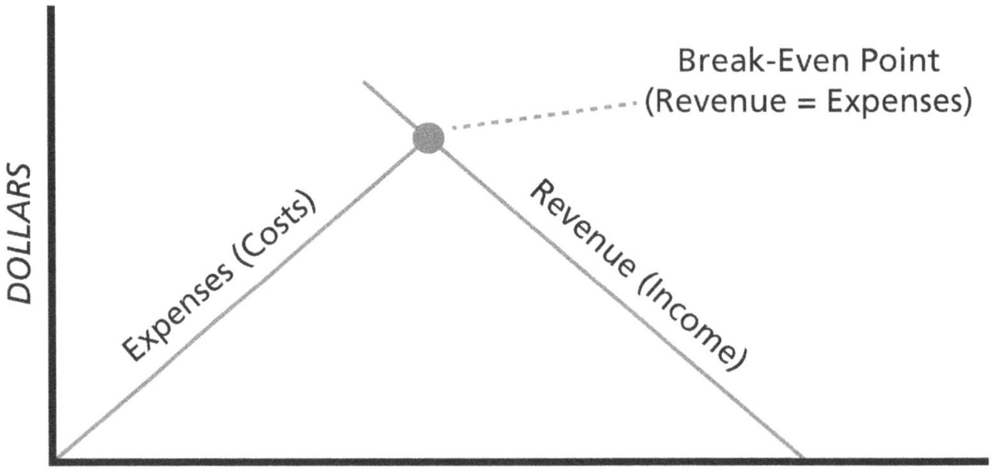

FIGURE 5.1
The break-even point.

Projecting Expenses

One aspect of generating an operating budget is projecting expenses. To project expenses, many organizations now use rolling forecasts, monthly reforecasting, or a different cadence (e.g., 9 + 3, 6 + 6). If you are not already familiar with monthly forecast variance narratives or any approach other than just simple annual budget-building, this is an area on which to focus on improving your knowledge.

After it calculates actual expenses, the organization identifies any expenses that should be omitted from the projection. These include:

- Expenses in excess of the budget that are not considered to be reasonable

- One-time expenses that are not expected to occur in the next budget year
- Prior-year expenses unrelated to current operating expenses

Estimated economic factors are also considered. While in limited contexts inflation/market assumptions may be developed by a state department of health, typically they are developed by internal finance, consultants, or standard indices. Nurse managers should ask what's baked into the labor assumptions: market adjustments, premium pay expectations, contract labor, benefit trend, supply inflation?

- Salaries
- Benefits
- Supplies
- Pharmaceuticals
- Food

NOTE

Often, estimated economic factors only reflect inflation rather than increased rates.

In any healthcare organization, nurse staffing generally takes the biggest bite out of the budget. Given current economic trends and the need to contain costs, nurse managers must increase productivity and work efficiency by staffing according to the planned hours of nursing care and by not exceeding those hours of care. This means continuously adjusting staffing to respond to both the patient census and the acuity of patients.

Productive Versus Nonproductive Nursing Hours

Productive nursing hours are hours worked in support of patient care. Understanding your organization's definitions for productive, nonproductive, worked, and paid hours is critical because dashboards vary widely. Examples of supporting patient care include:

- Administering a medication
- Planning a patient's treatment
- Administering a patient's treatment
- Admitting a patient
- Transferring a patient
- Discharging a patient
- Educating a patient
- Communicating with a patient
- Coordinating patient care
- Documenting patient care (either by hand or electronically)
- Reviewing charts

Example of Productive Work Hours

Recently, a hospital implemented Jean Watson's theory of caring and relationship-based care. This prompted one nursing unit to adopt a "caring moment" practice. With this practice, nurses proactively spend 10 to 15 minutes each day explaining to patients what they will experience that day (for example, any tests or procedures), answering any questions patients might have, and addressing any concerns patients raise. The hospital considers the time nurses spend communicating with patients during these caring moments to be productive hours worked.

In addition to productive nursing hours, there are nonproductive nursing hours. These include:

- Holiday time
- Vacation time
- Sick time
- Family/medical/personal leave time
- Bereavement time
- Orientation/education time
- Committee time

NOTE

Orientation/education time and committee time will vary by organization. Some organizations consider these to be productive work hours. It is important to consider this when there is a shared governance structure, as frontline nurses are required to participate in a number of committee meetings that should not be included in the productive hours.

Calculating Employee-Related Costs

The nursing department is usually the largest cost center in any hospital. Given that and the fact that the provision of healthcare is a service industry, it should come as no surprise that employees account for the greatest expense in a healthcare organization. For this reason, budget preparation in a healthcare setting usually starts with employees.

Before you begin, you'll want some key figures on hand. These include:

- **ADC for the responsibility center:** As mentioned, the ADC is the number of patients cared for each day on average over a specific period of time. To obtain this figure, use the following formula:

  Total Census Figures ÷ Total Number of Days = ADC

- **Average monthly patient days:** To obtain this figure, multiply the ADC by the number of days in the calendar year (365), and divide the product of that calculation by the number of months in the calendar year (12), as in the following equation:

  ADC x 365 ÷ 12 = Average Monthly Patient Days

- **Number of hours of nursing care to be provided:** To calculate this, multiply the total patient days per year by the hours of care per patient per day to be budgeted, as in the following equation:

  Total Patient Days/Year x Hours of Care/Patient Day = Hours of Nursing Care to Be Provided

- **Hours of care per patient day:** This is the hours of nursing care provided per patient day (over a 24-hour period). You generally obtain this information from various healthcare associations that collect, tabulate, and report nursing data, often on a statewide basis. This data typically includes hours of care per patient day, broken down by type of nursing unit (for example, medical-surgical, critical care, and so on).

- **Hours of care per patient day to be budgeted:** To obtain this figure, you multiply the hours of care per patient day by a value that reflects the standard of care you want to provide (determined by the nurse manager, chief nursing officer, and budget manager). This standard of care value reflects the nursing personnel you want to use—RN, LPN, nursing care tech, and so on—based on patient acuity. See the following equation:

Hours of Nursing Care Provided/Patient Day x Standard of Care Value (Levels of Nursing Personnel Needed) = Hours of Care/ Patient/Day to Be Budgeted

- As mentioned earlier, do not be fooled by the "label" on each unit. One ICU is not the same as another, and an urban trauma center ED is different from a rural or community ED. Understanding the individual nuances is essential. For example, suppose one healthcare system recently merged with another. The units have the same "names"; however, the level of patient acuity differs. They are taking the time to understand each unit and align it with the National Database of Nursing Quality Indicators and other standards of care to ensure that both patients and staff have the appropriate level of resources.
- **Total hours of care delivered:** This is the total number of actual patient days during the course of one year, multiplied by the hours of care per patient day, as in the following equation:

Total Patient Days for One Year x Hours of Care/Patient Day = Total Hours of Care Delivered

Budgeting and Standards of Care

As mentioned, budgeting for hours of nursing care provided per patient day requires you to account for standards of care. One of the better indicators of this is patient acuity. In the past, nurses gauged patient acuity themselves. Often, these assessments were extremely subjective—and inaccurate. Nurses frequently listed patients as high acuity when in fact they were not. Today, most acuity systems are computerized and are more objective in nature. However, even these systems are not perfect, which is why some healthcare facilities elect not to use them.

Calculating the Number of FTEs Needed

With these figures in hand, your first task is to calculate how many full-time employees (FTEs) are needed in a given responsibility center to do the job. By definition, an FTE works 2,080 hours per year (in acute care hospitals, for example, typically 12-hour shifts, four days per week). So, to calculate the total FTE requirements, you divide the total hours of care to be delivered per year by the hours worked by one FTE per year (2,080), as in the following equation:

Total Hours of Care to Be Delivered/Year ÷ Hours Worked by One FTE/Year (2,080) = Number of FTEs Needed

For example, if the total hours of care to be delivered were 146,000, you would divide that number by 2,080 for a result of 70.192. In other words, 70.192 FTEs would be needed to provide 146,000 hours of care.

NOTE

More than one employee can compose one FTE. For example, two part-time employees, each working 20 hours, would compose 1.0 FTE.

Accounting for Benefit Time

There is a problem with the equation for calculating the number of FTEs needed: It does not account for employee benefit, or *nonproductive*, time. Examples of benefit time include:

- Holiday time
- Vacation time
- Sick time
- Family/personal/medical leave
- Bereavement time
- Education/conference hours

NOTE

Every organization administers productive and nonproductive time differently. For example, some consider time spent on such things as orientation and continuing education to be productive time. Others count such hours as nonproductive time because the staff person's hours must be covered productively by someone else.

Suppose a healthcare organization offers FTEs the following benefit time:

- 10 vacation days
- 10 holidays
- 10 sick days
- Three bereavement days

This adds up to 33 days off per year. So, when developing a budget, you should assume that every FTE will take all their benefit time in that fiscal year (even though a lot of employees do not).

When accounting for benefit time, you must convert the benefit days to hours. Some organizations convert benefit time to 8-hour equivalents for budgeting; others use scheduled hours. Nurse managers should ask finance/HR how PTO is budgeted in their system because it directly affects true coverage needs.

Total Number of Benefit Days x 8 = Total Benefit Hours

After you convert the benefit days to hours, you must subtract those benefit hours from the 2,080 hours generally worked by an FTE. This yields each FTE's productive hours worked, as in the following equation. In this example, employees' productive hours worked equals 264 subtracted from 2,080, or 1,816.

2,080 – Total Benefit Hours = Productive Hours Worked

Finally, to obtain the *real* number of FTEs needed, you must divide the total staffed hours by the total productive time (in hours). So, in this example, the equation would look like this:

$$146{,}000 \div 1{,}816 = 80.4$$

Obviously, 80.4 is a much higher number than the 70.192 noted in the preceding section! In other words, an additional 10 FTEs are required to cover for employees when they take their benefit time. If a nurse manager did not go this extra step, that nursing unit would always be short-staffed or would have to be covered by overtime staff or agency staff, which might not be in the budget.

Other Key Calculations

NOTE

Annual payroll costs are generally at least 70% of the total budget for nursing. Nursing is a service department, and therefore, payroll costs are the most significant dollars expended.

As you develop your budget, you'll need to keep a few other formulas in mind:

- **Annual nursing hours:** You calculate this figure by multiplying the projected patient days in a year by the hours of nursing care per patient per day, as in the following equation. The annual nursing hours translate to money when the average hourly salary rate is factored in.

Projected Patient Days x Hours of Nursing Care/Patient/Day = Annual Nursing Hours

- **Annual payroll costs:** To calculate this, multiply the average hourly rate by the annual staffed hours, as in the following equation. (Hourly rates are set by the human resources department, and the average per unit is calculated by the finance department.)

Average Hourly Rate x Annual Staffed Hours = Annual Payroll

- **Annual benefit costs:** To calculate this, multiply annual payroll costs by the benefit percentage (furnished by the human resources department), as in the following equation:

Average Payroll Costs x Benefit Percentage = Annual Benefit Costs

- **Total annual payroll costs:** You calculate this by adding the annual payroll costs with the annual benefit costs, as in the following equation. The total annual payroll costs are the largest piece of the nursing operating budget.

Annual Payroll Costs + Annual Benefit Costs = Total Annual Payroll Costs

NOTE

Every organization provides benefits, and these benefits involve a cost. In most healthcare organizations, the benefit package is somewhere between 25% and 30%—sometimes more. The actual number depends on the organization. When making a budget, the cost of employee benefits must be factored in because it is a significant dollar amount.

Putting It All Together

Table 5.1 shows a sample personnel budget for a nursing unit. Take note of the formulas next to certain items in the table.

TABLE 5.1 FIXED PERSONNEL BUDGET FOR NURSING UNIT

Total bed capacity	**50**
Projected occupancy	80%
Projected ADC	40
Projected annual patient days	14,600 (40 x 365 days/year)
Average nursing hours per patient day	10 hours/patient day/24-hour period
Annual nursing hours (staffed hours)	146,000 (14,600 x 10)
Average hourly wage	$30
Annual salary costs minus benefits	$4,380,000 (146,000 x 30)
Benefits at 30% salary costs	$1,314,000 (0.30 x 4,380,000)
Total annual personnel (payroll) costs	$5,694,000 (4,380,000 + 1,314,000)
Average monthly patient days	1,216.7 (14,600 ÷ 12)
Average monthly nursing hours	12,166.7 (146,000 ÷ 12)
Average monthly personnel costs	$474,500 (5,694,000 ÷ 12)

Table 5.2 shows a flexible budget. In this example, a manager prepared three budgets based on variable census levels. Take note of the bold items, which do not change regardless of the census.

TABLE 5.2 FLEXIBLE PERSONNEL BUDGET FOR NURSING UNIT

	Census X	**Census Y**	**Census Z**
Total bed capacity	**50**	**50**	**50**
Projected occupancy	70%	80%	90%
Projected ADC	**35**	**40**	**45**

	Census X	Census Y	Census Z
Projected annual patient days	12,775	14,600	16,425
Average nursing hours per patient day	**10**	**10**	**10**
Annual nursing hours (staffed hours)	127,750	146,000	164,250
Average hourly wage	$30	$30	$30
Annual salary costs minus benefits	$3,832,500	$4,380,000	$4,927,500
Benefits at 30% of salary costs	$1,149,750	$1,314,000	$1,478,250
Total annual personnel (payroll) costs	$4,982,250	$5,694,000	$6,405,750

Bold items do not change regardless of census data.

Outpatient Reimbursement

Payment for outpatient care represents a growing percentage of total patient revenue in most hospitals. This is especially true since the 2010 passage of the Patient Protection and Affordable Care Act (ACA), which called for a shift in focus from acute care and interventional services to health promotion and primary care.

Other factors have contributed to the increase in outpatient care. These include improvements in technology that allow providers to conduct more noninvasive or less-invasive procedures in an outpatient setting as well as the increased prevalence of managed care.

Outpatient care is generally characterized by higher volume and lower revenue. However, outpatient revenue—typically generated from radiology, laboratory, infusion, and other services, as well as some ancillary care that relates to hospital-based visits—can also be more difficult to estimate and analyze.

To address this, healthcare organizations have adopted the Outpatient Prospective Payment System (OPPS). This is similar to the diagnosis-related group system used by Medicare for inpatient hospital care. The OPPS classifies types of care into groups called Ambulatory Payment Classifications (APCs). Depending on the services rendered, a hospital may be paid for more than one APC encounter. Established fee schedules are payer-specific. Payment is made for services such as:

- Laboratory
- Radiology
- Emergency department
- Clinic visits
- Ambulatory categories

The fee schedule also includes a technical and a professional component. The technical fee schedule is for hospital services; the professional fee schedule is for physicians and other health providers who deliver services in an office-based setting or for hospital staff physicians and healthcare providers delivering such a service in a hospital outpatient setting. Items that are not listed or categorized in the established fee schedule will typically default to a percent of charges as a payment methodology.

Busting Budget Myths

When it comes to budgeting, myths abound. Here are some common budget myths:

> **TIP**
>
> *Attrition can help with the budget and the bottom line.*

- **The more money you spend this year, the more money will be allocated in your budget next year.** Based on current reimbursement trends, the opposite is true. That is, the more money a nurse manager spends this year, the *less* money will be allocated in next year's budget. Worse, by spending too much money, the nurse manager may actually be hastening the organization's demise.

- **Every vacant FTE position must be filled ASAP.** Once upon a time, filling every vacated FTE immediately was important. If the nurse manager failed to do this, the finance department would most likely eliminate that FTE in the next year's budget, assuming the position was unnecessary because it had not been filled. Today, a nurse manager views a vacated FTE as an opportunity to reduce expenses and keep the organization whole (financially speaking) without having to resort to layoffs.
- **Do not be under budget; otherwise, your budget for the next year will be decreased.** Again, once upon a time, this myth was reality. A nurse manager who managed their unit prudently usually got penalized in the end. The finance department would assume that, thanks to the nurse manager's level of competence, if the unit ran with less this year, it could do so next year. That's no longer the case. These days, a good, prudent nurse manager tries to run their unit under budget. Nurse managers have become much more effective at variance analysis and productivity, optimizing revenue over expenses.
- **The state will always bail you out.** Al admitted, "I had this feeling as a new nurse manager. Heck, I even had it as a nurse executive! I thought the government would never let a hospital close." Guess what? Local, state, and national governments *do* let hospitals close. Perhaps the best example is Saint Vincent Hospital in downtown Manhattan. No one could have dreamed that hospital would close, but it did. Daily it seems like more hospitals are in jeopardy, are losing money, or are declaring bankruptcy.

Summary

This chapter discussed:

- Key metrics in the operating budget
- Understanding expenses
- Calculating employee-related costs
- Outpatient reimbursement
- Busting budget myths

Capital Budgets

Capital budgets, which are an important part of long-range and strategic planning, are used to budget for major movable equipment and fixed assets. Items in a capital budget typically have a lifetime exceeding the year of purchase. They are generally major investments; it takes a long time to recover their costs. However, many organizations have different capitalization thresholds, asset categories, and accounting/finance policies for different types of equipment. For example, software and IT hardware may be treated differently than a new CT scanner.

Why is a separate budget required for capital purchases? Because items in capital budgets are expensive. Also, they usually are expected to last a long time. Perhaps most importantly, the return on the investment in capital items will be seen over several years, not just the year of purchase.

> *"Budgets are blueprints and priorities."*
> *–Kevin McCarthy*

Budgeting for Major Movable Equipment

Major movable equipment includes items that are expected to last for longer than one year but that will not be a permanent fixture in the organization. For example, computer hardware, which lasts four to five years on average, is considered major movable equipment. Other examples include:

- Automatic blood pressure machines
- CT scanners and MRI machines
- Portable cardiac transport monitors
- Automatic external defibrillators (AEDs)
- Stretchers and beds

Which capital items are placed in a budget depends on an organization's budgeting policies—specifically with regard to the minimum dollar amount of items that must be included in the budget. This minimum amount will vary from organization to organization. The total amount budgeted for major movable equipment will also vary from organization to organization.

NOTE

Information technology (IT)–related purchases are excellent examples of capital budget items, although some may be categorized as operating components instead. Most healthcare organizations spend significant amounts of money on IT. Capital planning for IT often includes infrastructure, cybersecurity, analytics, optimization, interoperability, cloud hosting, subscription licensing, and ongoing upgrade costs.

Budgeting for Fixed Assets

In addition to budgeting for major movable items, you must consider fixed assets. Fixed assets are stationary. They do not move. A renovation of a conference center might appear in the capital budget as a fixed asset, as might a new building. Organizations can also purchase real estate for current or future growth and development; such purchases are also considered fixed assets.

NOTE

Nurse managers would be involved with such budgeting if, for example, their nursing unit was going to be renovated.

Appreciating Items: Fixed Assets

Fixed assets often *appreciate*. That is, their value increases over time. An excellent example of a fixed asset that appreciates is a real estate purchase. Many hospitals purchase properties around the hospital campus, often for future expansion. Generally, although initial costs will likely be high, these real estate purchases will typically increase or appreciate in value over time.

Examples of Capital Expenditures

Capital expenditures include:

- **Capital investments:** This is money that is invested in the business with the intended result of producing income through earnings generated by the business over a period of several years. This money is expected to be used for capital expenditures rather than day-to-day operational expenses.
- **Long-term investments:** These are investments that a company intends to hold onto for longer than one year. Examples include stocks, bonds, and real estate.

- **Capital assets:** These include land and buildings.
- **Capital acquisitions:** This describes any capitalizable assets purchased for the business. For a healthcare organization, examples include equipment, buildings, or IT infrastructure. Day-to-day purchased services and supplies are not capital acquisitions.
- **Capital items:** As mentioned, examples of capital items include automatic blood pressure machines, CT scanners, MRI machines, portable cardiac transport monitors, AEDs, and stretcher beds.

In some organizations, any items over $1,000 should appear in the capital budget. In others, that dollar amount might range from $350 to $5,000. (This dollar amount tends to rise with inflation.)

NOTE

Organizations that place items costing less than $1,000 on the capital budget tend to be very fiscally conservative—not necessarily a bad thing in today's economy!

Why Develop a Capital Budget?

Why develop a capital budget? Lots of reasons. Here are a few:

- **To improve quality for patients/staff:** When equipment and technology are not replaced or updated, patients and staff can be negatively affected. Think about it: Would you want to undergo a test or other procedure that did not involve the latest technology?
- **To improve safety for patients/staff:** Generally, more state-of-the-art technology provides improved safety for patients and staff.
- **To add new or update current technology:** For example, you might purchase an item to bring the institution to the level of a state-of-the-art facility.

- **To improve productivity:** Better equipment and technology improve throughput, safety, quality of care, reliability, and staff sustainability and retention and reduce non-value work.
- **To replace an older item with a similar updated item:** As stated, failing to replace outdated equipment and technology can have a negative impact on patients and staff. This often happens when infusion pumps need replacement. It is important to consider the impact of replacing all at the same time from both a financial and safety perspective.

Developing the Capital Budget

Developing a capital budget is a matter of determining what capital purchases should be made. These purchases could be direct or indirect:

- **Direct purchases:** These have a clear impact on the care provided or the workload involved. An example of a direct purchase is a piece of healthcare-related equipment. When the equipment arrives and is put to use, the care provided is directly affected.
- **Indirect purchases:** These have an indirect impact on the care provided or the workload involved. Examples of indirect purchases include spare parts, maintenance materials (such as lubricants for machinery), and operating supplies. These purchases are often included in the additional capital purchase and then need to be budgeted in the subsequent years as part of the operational budget.

NOTE

With capital expenditures, organizations commit to a multi-year relationship. The longer the acquisition will be around, the more scrutiny will be applied to its purchase.

To determine what items to include in a capital budget, start by maintaining inventories of major movable equipment. Then, for each piece of equipment, ask the following questions:

- What is the expected useful life of this piece of equipment?
- What is its anticipated depreciation value (see the next section)?
- How often is this piece of equipment used?
- Is this piece of equipment outdated?
- When was this equipment last replaced?
- When should this equipment be replaced again?

Answering these questions will help you determine when various pieces of equipment should be budgeted for in the capital budget.

In addition, you should survey your staff. Ask them what equipment they believe is necessary to do their job, improve patient care, and ensure their own safety. Nurse managers must retain staff, so capital items that help nurses do their job better or otherwise benefit them are often worth pursuing.

NOTE

It is not unusual for a capital purchase to result in a couple years of negative cash flow. However, cash flow impact depends on timing, financing method, reimbursement, and whether the purchase drives revenue or cost avoidance. ROI and cash flow impact vary widely by asset type as well (replacement vs. growth, revenue-generating vs. safety-driven).

When considering an item for the capital budget, managers must examine alternatives. That is, they must determine whether a similar item could be purchased for less money or if there might be other, less expensive ways to achieve the same results. Successful capital budgets evaluate alternative plans and purchases. The capital budget should not be just a wish list of items.

Perhaps most importantly, a purchase should yield a tangible economic return. When evaluating an item, ask these questions:

- Will the capital purchase price be offset by the anticipated revenue from the purchase?
- What will be the clinical impact of the capital acquisition?
- Is there a quality issue here? That is, does the purchase price exceed the proposed revenue but improve the overall quality of care?
- What will be the impact of the purchase on the staff?
- Will the staff's work life improve as a result of the purchase?
- Will labor hours be saved a result of the purchase?
- Will the purchase help make money for the organization?

Inevitably, you'll have to justify items in your capital budget to personnel in your facility's finance department and/or to a capital review committee. When the time comes, you want the following information on hand:

- A description of the item, including the name of the manufacturer and supplier
- The cost of the item
- Why you believe the purchase is necessary
- The impact of the item on the unit's or organization's operating revenues and expenses

NOTE

Boards of directors often appoint a capital review committee. *The purpose of this committee is to review all capital purchases. The capital review committee also monitors building and renovation projects undertaken by the organization to avoid exceeding budgeted dollars for such projects.*

Understanding Depreciation

Capital items depreciate over time. When budgeting capital items, you must consider the depreciation value. *Depreciation* spreads the cost of an item out over each useful year of an item's life. Although the capital acquisition itself will appear in the capital budget only in the year it is purchased, the depreciation costs will be identified in each year's operating budget for the life of the item.

The nurse manager can obtain information about depreciation in a couple ways:

- **The item's manufacturer may indicate the item's expected lifetime.** For example, it is generally accepted that computer technology must be replaced every four to five years or so due to changes in technology and the expected shelf life of most computers.
- **The organization may define the item's expected lifetime.** This happens when the depreciation time for an item is not established or is unclear. This time frame may be based on what the organization can afford over time.

NOTE

Nurse managers should first check with the manufacturer to see what the expected life of a piece of equipment is. The nurse manager can also check with the finance budget manager.

Although equipment may last a long time, the guidelines for their use may change, thus necessitating a change in the depreciation time and value. This often happens with IV pumps. It is important to work with pharmacy to ensure that the most up-to-date medication library is installed and that the parameters that are set align with organizational policies and procedures.

Capital Budget Major Movable Equipment Depreciation Example

Healthcare organizations generally base their equipment decisions on a couple of factors:

- Depreciation value
- Useful life of the item

Over time, most items depreciate in monetary value as well as useful life.

For the purposes of comparison, suppose you buy a refrigerator. If the refrigerator costs $2,000 and is expected to last around 10 years, then it depreciates $200 each year. So, ideally, you should plan to save $200 a year for 10 years so that if the refrigerator stops working after that period of time, you will have saved enough money to purchase a new one. When planning a capital budget for major movable equipment, most organizations now use condition-based replacement and risk-based prioritization (safety, failure rate, supportability, parts availability, cybersecurity, obsolescence) to determine purchasing and replacement rather than automatic replacement at "end of useful life."

Table 6.1 provides an example of a major movable equipment item in a capital budget that costs $1,000. The item described has an expected useful life of five years, so ideally, in year 5, a replacement item should be included in the capital budget.

TABLE 6.1 ITEM DEPRECIATION SCHEDULE

Year of Purchase Cost	Year 1 Depreciation	Year 2 Depreciation	Year 3 Depreciation	Year 4 Depreciation	Year 5 Depreciation	Total Depreciation Value in Year 5
$1,000	$200	$200	$200	$200	$200	$1,000

In this scenario, the plan would be to purchase a new item in year 5.

Planning Ahead for the Following Year

If you're responsible for developing a capital budget, you want to get into the habit of thinking ahead. In addition to building your budget for this year, start a list for the following year, too. For example, if you've proposed an item for this year's capital budget but that item has been deemed nonessential in the short term, you might add that item to your capital budget for the following year, at which point its purchase will become more critical.

Including a Contingency Line

It's a good idea to have a *contingency line* built into the capital budget for emergency items. The purpose of the contingency line is to cover items that absolutely must be purchased during the year but, for some reason, were not included in the capital budget (so-called "surprise items"). It's always better to ask to spend budgeted dollars than to request items that were not budgeted for—hence the contingency line! Many organizations use a percentage-based contingency or governance-defined reserve amount.

Contingency funds might also be used for non-emergency items. An example might be new technology—often very expensive—that becomes available after the budget is put in place. This happened to me a few times as director in one organization. After a few years, I learned to ask about the plans for contingency to help anticipate unexpected expenses. As CNO, I was fortunate to have a CEO who planned for contingency and monitored it consistently.

Applying Capital Budget Principles for Household Items That You Purchase

Consider this for home expenses. For example, you need to purchase a new washing machine. You go shopping and narrow your choice down to two machines: one that costs $500 and has a shelf life of five years and one that costs $1,500 and has an expected shelf life of 10 years.

After doing some quick math, you determine that if you purchase the $500 machine and spend another $500 to replace it in five years, you will pay only $1,000 over a 10-year period. In contrast, if you purchase the $1,500 machine, which has an expected life of 10 years, it would cost you $500 more over that same period. Put another way, if you bought the $500 machine, you would replace it every five years for 15 years for the same price as buying the $1,500 machine, which would likely last only 10 years. Not surprisingly, you decide to purchase the $500 machine. The added benefit is that as machine technology changes, you have an immediate upgrade!

Summary

This chapter covered:

- Budgeting for major movable equipment
- Budgeting for fixed assets
- Examples of capital expenditures
- Developing the capital budget
- Including a contingency line

Budget Variances

In general terms, *variance analysis* involves comparing the budgeted amount for an item with the actual amount spent to identify fiscal variances. The purpose of variance analysis is to pinpoint the cause of such fiscal variances. Armed with this knowledge, the nurse manager can take corrective action to prevent such occurrences in the future.

> *"In manufacturing we try to stamp out variance. With people, variance is everything."*
>
> *–Jack Welch*

NOTE

You can't undo what has already been done, but you can take corrective action to improve operational and fiscal performance going forward.

Conducting Variance Analysis

When conducting variance analysis, you analyze variances in the following three areas:

- **Efficiency:** Also known as the *quantity variance* or *use variance*. In this context, efficiency variances reflect how accurately the nurse manager budgeted for care hours provided. For example, suppose a nurse manager budgets for *x* number of care hours per day, but the actual number turns out to be higher. The result would be a negative efficiency and budget variance (unless the increased nursing care hours were due to increased volume) because more care hours provided translates to more money spent on staffing.
- **Volume:** This relates to the number of patients for whom care was provided. Generally, increased patient volume means both increased revenue and increased cost. When volume increases, nurse managers need more staff to provide the same number of nursing hours per patient day.
- **Cost:** Cost variances relate to how many dollars are spent to deliver care. If a nurse manager were to provide more hours of care than were budgeted, the additional staffing to provide that care would likely be paid in overtime, agency, or bonus dollars, resulting in a higher cost to deliver the care.

Understanding Bonus or Incentive Dollars

Bonus/incentive dollars are generally funds paid to entice employees to work extra hours, whether they are part-time or full-time employees. Overtime rules vary by jurisdiction and by employer policy (and some organizations have daily overtime rules, shift-based differentials, or contract language), so nurse managers need to be knowledgeable of their local policy, union terms, and payroll rules. Overtime and premium pay treatment is one of the most common real-world variance drivers.

NOTE

Calculating efficiency, volume, and cost variances improves your ability to diagnose problems and identify corrective measures to improve performance.

Calculating Variances

Table 7.1 shows a sample budget report from a one-month period.

TABLE 7.1 SAMPLE BUDGET REPORT

	Budget	Actual	Budget Variance
Patient days	425	499	74
Nursing care hours	1,790	2,290	500
Average hourly pay rate	$40/hour	$45/hour	$5/hour
Total payroll costs	$56,925	$88,791	$31,866

As you can see, this nursing unit's total payroll costs are $31,866 over the budgeted amount of $56,925. Let's analyze the three critical items—efficiency, volume, and cost—to determine whether this variance is a cause for concern.

Step 1: Calculating the Efficiency Variance

To calculate the efficiency variance for the sample budget report shown in Table 7.1, follow these steps:

1. Calculate the budgeted hours per patient day (HPPD) using the following formula:

Budgeted Nursing Care Hours ÷ Budgeted Patient Days = Budgeted HPPD

For the sample budget report in Table 7.1, the budgeted HPPD is as follows:

1,790 ÷ 425 = 4.2

2. Calculate the actual HPPD using the following formula:

Actual Nursing Care Hours ÷ Actual Patient Days = Actual HPPD

For the sample budget report, the actual HPPD is as follows:

2,290 ÷ 499 = 4.6

3. Use the following formula to calculate the average extra nursing care hours:

Actual HPPD – Budgeted HPPD = Average Extra Nursing Care Hours

For the sample budget report, the average extra nursing care hours are as follows:

4.6 – 4.2 = 0.4

4. Use the following formula to calculate the total number of extra nursing care hours:

Actual Patient Days x Average Extra Nursing Care Hours = Total Extra Nursing Care Hours

For the sample budget report, the total extra nursing care hours are as follows:

499 x 0.4 = 199.6

5. Use the following formula to calculate the efficiency variance:

Total Extra Nursing Care Hours x Budgeted Average Hourly Pay Rate = Efficiency Variance

For the sample budget report, the efficiency variance is as follows:

199.60 x $40 = $7,984

Step 2: Calculating the Volume Variance

Calculating the volume variance involves a similar series of formulas. To calculate the volume variance for the sample budget report shown in Table 7.1, follow these steps:

1. Calculate the number of extra patient days using the following formula:

   Actual Patient Days – Budgeted Patient Days = Extra Patient Days

   For the sample budget report in Table 7.1, the extra patient days are as follows:

   499 – 425 = 74

2. Use the following formula to calculate the extra nursing care hours provided:

   Extra Patient Days x Budgeted HPPD = Extra Nursing Care Hours Provided

   For the sample budget report, the extra nursing care hours provided are as follows:

   74 x 4.2 = 310.80

3. Use the following formula to calculate the volume variance:

   Extra Nursing Care Hours Provided x Budgeted Average Hourly Pay Rate = Volume Variance

   For the sample budget report, the volume variance is as follows:

   310.80 x $40 = $12,432

Step 3: Calculating the Cost Variance

Calculating the cost variance is quite simple. To calculate the cost variance for the sample budget report shown in Table 7.1, follow these steps:

1. Use the following formula to calculate the cost difference:

   Actual Average Hourly Pay Rate – Budgeted Average Hourly Pay Rate = Hourly Cost Difference

   For the sample budget report in Table 7.1, the hourly cost difference is as follows:

   $45 – $40 = $5

2. Use the following formula to calculate the cost variance:

   Hourly Cost Difference x Actual Nursing Care Hours = Cost Variance

   For the sample budget report, the cost variance is as follows:

   $5 x 2,290 = $11,450

NOTE

If the budgeted average hourly pay rate is less than the actual average hourly pay rate, the result of this calculation will be a positive number. If the budgeted average hourly pay rate is more than the actual average hourly pay rate, the result will be a negative number. In this example, the actual average hourly rate paid is more than the budgeted average hourly rate, so the result will be a positive number.

Putting It All Together

As a final step, add these three variances—the efficiency, volume, and cost variances—together to calculate the total variance:

Efficiency Variance + Volume Variance + Cost Variance = Total Variance

For the sample budget report in Table 7.1, the total variance is as follows:

$7,984 + $12,432 + $11,450 = $31,866

Notice that the total variance shown here ($31,866) matches the total variance shown in Table 7.1. The numbers in the variance analysis demonstrate that volume and cost are the primary variance drivers.

The question becomes, was this over-budget amount justified? Most new nurse managers would argue that it was, simply because the number of patient days increased by 74 (regardless of whether this increase in fact contributed to the overage). In reality, though, a bit more analysis is needed. It is not good enough to simply go with your gut!

For today's nurse managers, increased volume is not automatically a positive development because it could affect capacity constraints, throughput/LOS dynamics, payer mix, and staffing availability, and/or have quality and safety impacts. Volume is a variance driver to understand, even if it can't always be controlled. Nurse managers should partner with finance/throughput teams to interpret whether the volume change is beneficial (e.g., growth) or operationally problematic (e.g., extended LOS).

Assessing Efficiency Variance

With respect to the efficiency variance, nurse managers should consider the following:

- Can staffing be made more flexible based on actual volumes?
- Is the appropriate skill mix being used?
- Looking at prior reports, does this nursing unit consistently run over budget?
- Is the unit classified correctly, and are the HPPD/HPPV reflective of the patient acuity?

NOTE

If prior reports show that this unit is consistently over budget, it could be that this year's budget failed to allot enough care hours.

Nurse managers should also compare available data—for example, nursing care hours per patient per day—for similar units in similar healthcare organizations. This information can assist nurse managers in designing the budget for the following year. Fortunately, many hospitals, nursing homes, and other health facilities belong to national and/or statewide organizations that collect this type of data. I frequently use these reports to benchmark our own nursing care hours per patient day. However, it is important to review the unit classifications. For example, one telemetry unit may be straight telemetry and no titrating medication drips, while another may titrate medications. While both may be labeled telemetry, clearly one handles more complex patients. Another area may be an intensive care unit. Is the unit all medical, all surgical, or is it combined? Again, know your patient acuity so that you can benchmark at the appropriate levels.

Assessing Cost Variance

With cost variance, nurse managers should consider the following:

- Have there been changes in wages that were not budgeted?
- Is the appropriate staff skill mix being used?
- Has more costly labor—for example, float pool, bonus, or agency labor—been used?
- Is there a need to fill existing vacancies?

NOTE

It is not a great cause for concern if the cost variance is due to higher volume. If efficiency and cost variances increase but volume decreases, however, it is a cause for concern.

Avoiding Negative Cost Variances

There are two main reasons for negative cost variances:

- The unit is overstaffed, increasing the total nursing hours per patient day.
- Staff shortages have forced nurse managers to use overtime, bonus pay, or agency nursing to fill in the gaps.

Here are some ways to prevent negative variances so you can improve efficiency and control costs:

- If additional staffing is warranted due to increased volume, see whether a nurse can be reassigned from a nursing unit with decreased volume. (Of course, the reassigned nurse must have the skills needed to work on the different unit.)
- Consider whether a lower-paid employee can be utilized—for example, a patient care technician rather than a registered nurse.
- Consider developing an as-needed float pool.
- Track volume on a daily basis to identify the busiest times on the nursing unit and schedule your staff accordingly. For example, if your busiest time is from noon to 8 p.m., consider scheduling one or more nurses or nursing assistants for an eight-hour shift during that busy period (even if your other nurses work 12-hour shifts).

- Balance full-time staff with a decent complement of part-time nurses. If additional staff are needed due to either increased volume or patient acuity, try to have part-time nurses work extra, as this should not involve overtime pay.
- Review timely budget reports. If a nursing unit consistently exhibits negative variances, analyze the reports to see what is causing the problem so you can take corrective action. If the negative variances are due to increases in patient acuity or volume, it may be time to meet with the budget manager and chief nursing officer to add more staff.

Variances in a Pandemic

A pandemic will cause significant variances in operations. This was certainly true of the COVID-19 pandemic. During a pandemic, variances occur for several reasons. These include:

- Increased volume
- Increased patient acuity (patients on ventilators), requiring increased nursing care hours per patient day
- Increased dollars spent due to increased staffing and supply costs

Regarding increased dollars spent due to increased staffing, when a hospital's ICU reaches maximum capacity, such was the case with COVID-19 patients, that hospital must set up additional ICU space on a temporary basis and bring in additional trained staff. In some of our hardest-hit areas, hospitals and other healthcare facilities have had to rely on agency nurses and traveling nurses from other states. In addition, frontline workers must be paid appropriately for the increased risks that they are taking, often in the form of bonus pay. All this costs money and increases budget variances.

NOTE

During the COVID-19 pandemic, governors in many states issued executive orders to allow nurses who are licensed in other states to practice in their (the governors') states. Since then, many of these orders have expired, and post-pandemic mobility is more often managed through formal mechanisms (e.g., interstate compacts) than emergency orders. For example, the Nurse Licensure Compact (NLC/eNLC) allows nurses to obtain one multistate license so they can practice in their resident state as well as in the more than 40 state participants, for both in-person care and telehealth (National Council of State Boards of Nursing, 2026).

To keep up with demand during a pandemic or other acute circumstances, organizations must also provide the following for their staff:

- **Financial incentives:** Examples of this might be higher hourly wages and bonus pay. Other examples could include free uniforms, laundering, parking, meals, and so on.
- **Mental health services:** This could include free counseling for employees.
- **General support systems:** These could include time off, support and encouragement from leaders, small incentives such as free coffee and donuts, and other ideas to further support staff.

NOTE

Among the many individuals I interviewed on the topic of operating a hospital or healthcare facility during a pandemic, there was a resounding theme that patient and staff safety was priority #1.

Summary

This chapter covered:

- Conducting variance analysis
- Calculating variances
- Assessing efficiency variance
- Assessing cost variance
- Avoiding negative cost variances
- Pandemic-related variances

"The analysis of variance is not a mathematical theorem, but rather a convenient way of arranging the arithmetic."

–Ronald A. Fisher

Reference

National Council of State Boards of Nursing. (2026). *About the NLC.* https://www.nursecompact.com/about.page

Budget Reports

Understanding and using budgets to effectively manage resources is critical, especially given the driving economic forces and constraints and the relentless focus on cost-effectiveness and quality care by healthcare organizations. The budget needs to be a tool that managers use to *act*.

For this to be possible, reports are necessary. Reports provide nurse managers with extremely valuable information. With reports, you can track patterns and trends and perform variance analyses. Armed with this information, you can take necessary corrective measures to improve performance in upcoming budget cycles.

> *"When I take a look at a company's report, if I don't understand it, they don't want me to understand it."*
>
> *–Warren Buffett*

NOTE

Reports must be viewed in a timely manner to be effective.

Types of Budget Reports

There are many types of budget reports—some reports generated annually, some monthly, and some biweekly.

Annual reports in a healthcare organization might include the following:

- **Personnel budget worksheet:** This worksheet lists personnel budget expense items. It is used by nurse managers.
- **Supply and expense budget worksheet:** This worksheet lists supplies and related expenses. It is used by nurse managers.
- **Budget distribution report:** This report is distributed to responsibility center managers.

Monthly reports in a healthcare organization might include the following:

- **Actual to budget comparison:** This report compares actual expenses during the specified time period with budgeted expenses.
- **Cost distribution:** This report reveals the cost distribution, also known as the distribution cost. This can be defined generically as costs distributed across different product lines in healthcare—especially shared or indirect costs so that each cost center/department bears a fair and proportional share of the expenses. This often occurs for corporate services such as quality, risk, and information technology.
- **Inventory monthly distribution:** This is a monthly distribution report for inventory. This report is used to control inventory.
- **Payroll position control listing:** This report lists what employee positions have been filled and what vacancies exist. The HR department and nursing managers use this report to avoid hiring too many staff—that is, to *not* hire staff when all positions have already been filled.

Biweekly reports in a healthcare organization might include the following:

- **Detailed departmental summary:** This report summarizes activities for a given period for a nursing unit or department.
- **Employees not working authorized hours:** This report lists employees who did not work scheduled hours—for example, if an employee is on vacation, medical leave, or family medical leave of absence.

In addition to these, there are reports that pertain specifically to staffing. These are discussed in more detail in the next section.

Real-World Example: Customized Reports

If your organization permits it, consider working with colleagues in the finance department to develop customized reports tailored to meet your specific needs. For example, a nurse manager might want a customized report so they can better manage a budget.

I always found it valuable to partner with the CFO so they understood our lingo as I worked to understand theirs. It is not uncommon for them to use terms that are unfamiliar to us. One day I asked our CFO how the new hand sanitizer impacted his integumentary system. He asked me if that was part of his computer! Just a small example, but it made an impact.

Financial Reports

Financial reports identify revenue generated and expenses incurred over a period of time—often for one calendar month or a 28-day period. Such reports display the total for the year to date (YTD) for the unit, department, and organization. Items are sorted into groups and reported by accounts. Expenses are generally sorted into employment costs and non-salary expenses. These reports typically show the actual and budgeted revenues and expenses for the month and YTD, as well as any variances.

Many organizations also use 13-period fiscal years, 4-4-5 calendars, and near-real-time dashboards. Nurse managers increasingly interact with dashboards plus month-end finance, not just static monthly reports. Therefore, managers may see monthly close + periodic/fiscal-cycle reporting + interim dashboards in their organizations.

Examples of Staff Reports

This section presents several examples of staff reports. These include comparative staff summary reports, comparative staffing reports, a mix analysis report, a nursing care hour report, and a nursing salary variance report.

Example 1: Comparative Staff Summary Report 1

Let's start with the comparative staff summary report shown in Table 8.1. This report is for pay period 16 at Hospital X. (In this organization, pay periods run biweekly.) It contains statistical data about the following items:

- Beds in service
- Admissions
- Patient days
- Length of stay
- Average daily census
- Percent occupancy
- FTE (staffed)
- Hours (staffed)
- Hours per patient day (HPPD)

TABLE 8.1 COMPARATIVE STAFF SUMMARY REPORT 1

PAY PERIOD 16 NURSING STATION: 3RD		CSSPRT PROCESS DATE: 08/22/25	
STATISTICAL DATA	**2025 BUDGET**	**2025 ACTUAL PAY PERIOD**	**2025 ACTUAL YTD PAY PERIOD 16**
BEDS IN SERVICE	39	39	39
ADMISSIONS	55	52	810
PATIENT DAYS	519	479	8,123
LENGTH OF STAY	9.4	9.2	10
AVERAGE DAILY CENSUS	37	34	36
PERCENT OCCUPANCY %	95.1	87.7	93
FTE (STAFFED)	33	37.1	35.8
HOURS (STAFFED)	2,641.0	2,965.0	45,918.5
HOURS/PATIENT DAY	5.1	6.2	5.7

This report details the following:

- The budget for this pay period
- The YTD performance (i.e., what has actually occurred during the first 16 pay periods)

When analyzing this report, you can see the following:

- The budgeted hours of care per patient day were 5.1 hours. During the 16th pay period, however, the unit actually delivered 6.2 hours of care per patient day. Thus, this nursing unit was over by 1.1 care HPPD. You might say to yourself, "No big deal." But if every nursing unit were over by this number of care hours, there would be severe financial consequences for the organization.

- The YTD care hours are 5.7. So, overall, the unit is 0.6 care hours over budget. If the trend of delivering more care hours on a biweekly basis continues, the YTD hours could be significantly over budget by year's end.

NOTE

To review, you calculate the actual nursing care hours (here, 6.2 per patient per day) by dividing the hours staffed (2,965.2) by the patient days (479). However, make sure you understand how your organization defines "hours staffed." Many organizations distinguish productive hours (direct care) and paid hours (including orientation, education, professional development, and PTO), so make sure you are calculating HPPD in the manner consistent with your finance department.

The appropriate thing to do here is to conduct a variance analysis to see what is causing the unit to go over budget. However, you can garner a lot from the report itself. Specifically, according to the report, both admissions and patient days are down. That is, there were 55 admissions budgeted but only 52 actual admissions for this pay period. In addition, although there were 519 patient days budgeted, there were only 479 actual patient days for this pay period. This may be one driver of the over-budget situation. However, you should also consider skill mix, premium/incentive pay, increased acuity, sitter usage, and other productivity metrics also shown in the report as possible contributing drivers.

Example 2: Comparative Staff Summary Report 2

The comparative staff summary report in Table 8.2 shows statistical data about the same set of items as the report in Table 8.1. However, instead of showing data from a specific pay period in a single year, it contains historical data from that same pay period over three years.

TABLE 8.2 COMPARATIVE STAFF SUMMARY REPORT 2

PAY PERIOD 16 NURSING STATION: 3RD			COMPARATIVE STAFFING SUMMARY	
STATISTICAL DATA	**2022 ACTUAL**	**2023 ACTUAL**	**2024 ACTUAL**	**2025 ACTUAL**
BEDS IN SERVICE	39	39	39	39
ADMISSIONS	1,158	1,158	1,259	1,359
PATIENT DAYS	13,392	13,647	13,749	12,807
LENGTH OF STAY	11.6	11.8	10.9	9.4
AVERAGE DAILY CENSUS	37	37	38	35
PERCENT OCCUPANCY %	94.1	95.9	96.6	90.0
FTE (STAFFED)	34.9	35.4	36.6	35.5
HOURS (STAFFED)	72,482	73,641	76,022	73,913
HOURS/PATIENT DAY	5.7	5.4	5.5	5.18

This report not only provides information about current operations but also serves as a great tool for planning services and budgets in the future. For example, through 2025, the average daily census and patient days were increasing. If that trend were to continue, you would likely need to increase staffing levels in future budgets to deliver the budgeted nursing care hours.

Notice that this report calculates the average length of stay. This is the first time that this formula is discussed. To calculate the average length of stay, you use the following equation:

Patient Days in a Given Period ÷ Number of Admissions During That Period = Average Length of Stay

For example, the average length of stay in 2025 was as follows:

12,807 ÷ 1,359 = 9.4

Example 3: Comparative Staff Summary Report 3

The comparative staff summary report shown in Table 8.3 details the levels of staffing based on skill level used in this particular nursing unit. A comparison is made between budgeted and actual staffing for pay period 16.

Highlights of this report include the following:

- This report shows that 0.1 productive hours are budgeted for the department head or supervisor. In a two-week period, this would equate to 1.4 hours of care being provided by the department head. The report correctly does not count the administrative functions of this job toward the HPPD.
- This unit used no agency staff during this period.
- In actuality, roughly 60% of the care on this unit is provided by RNs. This unit also uses LPNs, nursing aides, clerical staff, and orderlies.
- The actual care hours provided exceed the budgeted care hours provided. The FTEs are also over budget for this period.
- Total overtime hours are below budget for this period.
- The actual productive hours per patient day (PRD HR/PAT DAY) were over budget for this period.

Example 4: Comparative Staffing Report 1

The comparative staffing report shown in Table 8.4 is identical to the comparative staffing report shown in Table 8.3, except this report shows the actual YTD figures through the 16 pay periods. Nurse managers and CNOs benefit from such reports because they demonstrate whether the staffing is in line with budgeted nursing care HPPD. The report also shows the amount of overtime used by staff categories—registered nurse, licensed practical nurse, and so on. When there is an excess of overtime, common drivers can be that a lot of staff are on a family leave of absence, there is limited internal float coverage, or there are other staffing market constraints. Or it might

TABLE 8.3 COMPARATIVE STAFF SUMMARY REPORT 2

	PAY PERIOD											
STAFFING DATA	BUDGET						PAY PERIOD 16					
SKILL LEVEL	FTE	TOTAL HOURS	OT	OTHER	PROD HOURS	PRD HR/ PAT DAY	FTE	TOTAL HOURS	OT	OTHER	PROD HOURS	PRD HR/ PAT DAY
.01 RN'S & GN'S	14.4	1,149	21	1,013	1,034	2	20.5	1,642.2	25.2	1,545.5	1,570.7	3.3
.02 LPN'S	11.9	955	12	848	860	1.7	9.9	789.2	10	749.8	759.8	1.6
.03 AIDES	2.7	216	8	186	194	0.4	1.5	120	0.0	111.0	111.0	0.2
.08 SUPR & DEPT HEADS	1	80	0	72	72	0.1	1	80	0.0	80	80	0.2
AGENCY	0	0	0	0	0	0.0	0.0	0.0	0.0	0.0	0.0	0.0
SUBTOTAL	**30**	**2,400**	**41**	**2,119**	**2,160**	**4.2**	**32.9**	**2,631.4**	**35.2**	**2,486.3**	**2,521.5**	**5.3**
.04 TECHNICIANS	0	0	0	0	0	0	0.0	0.0	0.0	0.0	0.0	0.0
.05 CLERICAL	2	160.0	8.0	136.0	144	0.3	3.2	253.8	2.9	205.2	208.1	0.4
.07 OTHER PROFESSIONALS	0	0	0	0	0	0	0	0	0.0	0.0	0.0	0.0
.09 ORDERLIES	1	81	2	71	73	0.1	1	80	0.0	80.0	80	0.2
TOTAL	**33**	**2,641**	**51**	**2,326**	**2,377**	**4.6**	**37.1**	**2,965.2**	**38.1**	**2,771.5**	**2,809.6**	**5.9**
							CALCULATED FTES: 37.1					

be because acuity or patient volume has increased. Again, nurse managers should carefully consider all drivers that may be present in the report, noting whether it is volume/acuity or workforce availability or coverage gap, or both.

TABLE 8.4 COMPARATIVE STAFF SUMMARY REPORT 1

STAFFING DATA		YTD PAY PERIOD				
SKILL LEVEL	**FTE**	**TOTAL HOURS**	**OT**	**OTHER**	**PROD HOURS**	**PRD HR/ PAT DAY**
.01 RN'S & GN'S	16.5	21,147.7	550.5	19,116.2	19,666.7	2.4
.02 LPN'S	12.6	16,083.3	486.2	13,916.5	14,402.7	1.8
.03 AIDES	2.2	2,778.3	68.5	2,469.3	2,537.8	0.3
.08 SUPR & DEPT HEADS	0.8	1,064.1	0	1,025.7	1,025.7	0.1
AGENCY	0.0	0	0	0	0	0.0
SUBTOTAL	**32.1**	**41,073.4**	**1,105.2**	**36,527.7**	**37,632.9**	**4.6**
.04 TECHNICIANS	0	0	0	0	0	0
.05 CLERICAL	3	3,889.6	18.4	3,483.7	3,502.1	0.4
.07 OTHER PROFESSIONALS	0	0	0	0	0	0
.09 ORDERLIES	0.7	955.5	11.9	832.5	844.4	0.1
TOTAL	**35.8**	**45,918.5**	**1,135.5**	**40,843.9**	**41,979.4**	**5.1**
		CALCULATED FTES: 35.8				

Example 5: Comparative Staffing Report 2

This report, shown in Table 8.5, is a report for a critical care unit. The report contains the same type of historical data and all the other items discussed in the preceding four reports. This report is for a different pay period, pay period 15. It puts everything together into one report format.

The CNO in an organization might generate such a report for each nursing unit and an overall summary report for the entire nursing division. Ideally, these reports would run every two weeks, when the biweekly payroll cycle runs. This would provide timely information, enabling nurse managers to take action to avoid overspending during the next two-week period.

TABLE 8.5 COMPARATIVE STAFF SUMMARY REPORT 2

COMPARATIVE STAFFING SUMMARY

CSSPRT

PAY PERIOD 16 — PROCESS DATE: 08/08/2025

NURSING STATION: 3RD — TIME: 11:31.03

STATISTICAL DATA	2023 ACTUAL	2024 ACTUAL	2025 BUDGET	2025 ACTUAL PAY PERIOD 15	2025 ACTUAL YTD PAY PERIOD 15
BEDS IN SERVICE	13	12	13	13	13
ADMISSIONS	497	446	20	10	175
PATIENT DAYS	4,042	4,099	150	176	2,572
LENGTH OF STAY	8.1	9.2	7.5	17.6	14.7
AVERAGE DAILY CENSUS	11	11	11	13	12
OCCUPANCY %	85.2	93.6	82.4	96.7	94.2
FTE (STAFFED)	35.7	41.3	44.8	43.3	42.7
HOURS (STAFFED)	6,713	2,161	0	0	0
HOURS/PATIENT DAY	20.0	21.5	23.9	19.7	19.9

STAFFING DATA	PAY PERIOD 15						YTD PAY PERIOD					
SKILL LEVEL	FTE	TOTAL HOURS	OT	OTHER	PROD HOURS	PRD HR/ PAT DAY	FTE	TOTAL HOURS	OT	OTHER	PROD HOURS	PRD HR/ PAT DAY
.01 RN'S & GN'S	35.9	2,873.4	243.0	2,322.4	2,565.4	14.6	34.1	40,878.0	4,110.2	33,081.5	37,191.7	14.5
.02 LPN'S	4.0	322.0	17.0	269.0	286.0	1.6	4.0	4,818.9	513.8	3,401.9	3,924.7	1.5
.03 AIDES	1.0	82.2	2.2	80.0	82.0	0.5	1.0	1,214.6	9.4	1,078.3	1,087.7	0.4
.08 SUPR & DEPT HEADS	1.0	80.0	0.0	79.5	79.5	0.5	1.9	2,246.9	0.0	2,013.8	2,013.8	0.8
AGENCY	0.0	0.0	0.0	0.0	0.0	0.0	0.0	0.0	0.0	0.0	0.0	0.0
SUBTOTAL	**41.9**	**3,357.6**	**262.2**	**2,750.9**	**3,013.1**	**17.2**	**41.0**	**49,158.4**	**4,633.4**	**39,584.5**	**44,217.9**	**17.2**
.04 TECHNICIANS	0.0	0.0	0.0	0.0	0.0	0.0	0.1	104.0	8.0	96.0	104.0	0.0
.05 CLERICAL	1.4	110.6	14.6	96.0	110.6	0.6	1.5	1,776.9	221.0	1,501.4	1,722.4	0.7
.07 OTHER PROFESSIONALS	0.0	0.0	0.0	0.0	0.0	0.0	0.0	12.0	0.0	12.0	12.0	0.0
.09 ORDERLIES	0.0	0.0	0.0	0.0	0.0	0.0	0.1	159.3	7.0	152.3	159.3	0.1
TOTAL	**43.3**	**3,468.2**	**276.8**	**2,846.9**	**3,123.7**	**17.8**	**42.7**	**51,210.6**	**4,869.4**	**41,346.2**	**46,215.6**	**18.0**
	CALCULATED FTES: 43.4						CALCULATED FTES: 42.7					

Example 6: Staff Mix Analysis Report

This report, shown in Table 8.6, illustrates the breakdown of actual care hours by skill level—for example, licensed vs. unlicensed assistive personnel, trainees/residents—compared to the standard care hours budgeted for this unit. The nurse manager and CNO use this information to analyze skill mix. They also use it to assess whether nursing care hours are in line with the budget or if they are exceeding budget thresholds for budgeted HPPD/skill mix targets.

Example 7: Nursing Care Hour Report

Someone once said that a picture is worth a thousand words. This is especially true of graphs, like the one in the nursing care hour report shown in Figure 8.1. This report contains a nice graph that compares actual hours delivered to the standard budgeted hours. This enables nurse managers to see at a glance whether they are in line with the budget, over budget, or under budget.

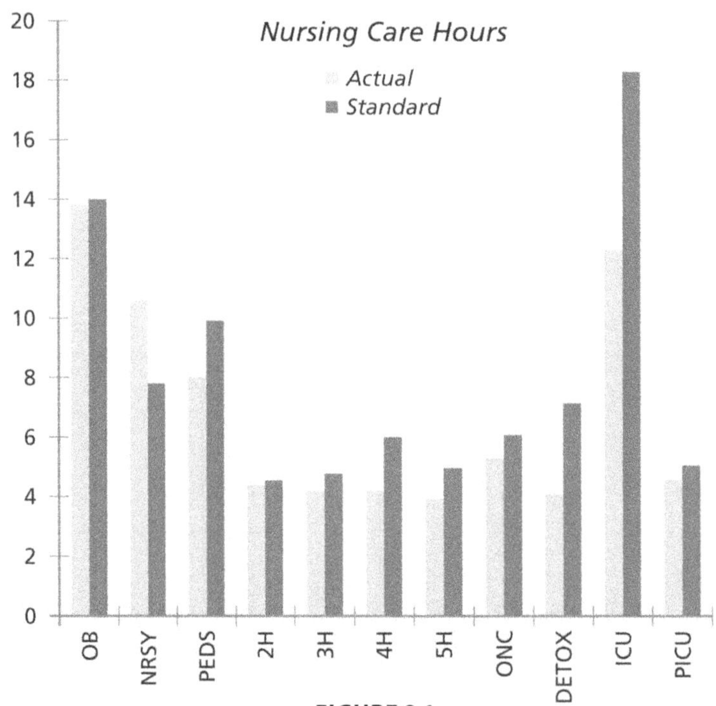

FIGURE 8.1
Nursing care hour report.

TABLE 8.6 STAFF MIX ANALYSIS REPORT

DATE:

ACTUAL vs STANDARD NURSING CARE HOURS

SHIFT	STANDARD N.C.H.	ACTUAL NURSING CARE HOURS								
		OB	PEDS	2H	3H	4H	5H	5S	5W	DETOX
7a-3p	2.0	2.1	7.2	1.6	1.9	3.1	1.9	2.0	4.0	1.0
3p-11p	1.5	~	~	1.4	2.1	1.8	1.5	1.6	4.0	1.8
11p-7a	1.0	3.5	8.0	1.0	1.1	1.5	1.0	1.2	4.0	2.0
TOTAL	**4.5**	**5.6**	**15.2**	**4.0**	**5.1**	**6.4**	**4.4**	**4.8**	**12.0**	**4.8**

SHIFT	ICU/CCU S.N.C.H.	A.N.C.H.	SHIFT	PICU S.N.C.H.	A.N.C.H.
7a-7p	7.5	8.3	7a-7p	3.75	4.2
7p-7a	7.5	10.2	7p-7a	3.75	2.9
TOTAL:	**15.0**	**18.5**	**TOTAL**	**7.5**	**7.1**

STAFF MIX ANALYSIS ICU/CCU, PICU

		RN	GN	LPN	ASST'S & AIDES	ORT'S
ICU/CCU	7a-7p	8	~	~	~	1
	7p-7a	6	~	2	~	3
PICU	7a-7p	3	~	3	~	1
	7p-7a	4	~	1	~	~

STAFF MIX ANALYSIS

		OB	PEDS	2H	3H	4H	5H	5S	5W	DETOX
RN	7a-3p	7	2	2	2	2	3	4	1	1
	3p-11p	~	~	3	3	3	3	4	1	2
	11p-7a	6	1	2	3	3	1	3	1	1
GN	7a-3p	~	~	2	~	~	~	~	~	~
	3p-11p	~	~	0.5	1	~	1	~	~	~
	11p-7a	~	~	2	~	~	~	~	~	~
LPN	7a-3p	1	1	1	5	2	3	2	1	1
	3p-11p	~	~	2	2.5	1	1	3	~	1
	11p-7a	2	1	1	1	1	3	2	~	1
GPN	7a-3p	~	~	~	~	~	~	~	~	~
	3p-11p	~	~	~	~	~	~	~	~	~
	11p-7a	~	~	~	~	~	~	~	~	~
ASST'S & AIDES	7a-3p	~	~	2	2	3	1	2	~	~
	3p-11p	~	~	1	1	2	1	~	~	~
	11p-7a	1	~	~	1	1	~	~	~	~
ORT'S	7a-3p	~	~	~	~	3	1	2	~	~
	3p-11p	~	~	~	1	~	~	1	~	~
	11p-7a	1	~	~	~	~	~	1		

S.N.C.H. = Standard Nursing Care Hours ***ANCH = staff X hours*** ***A.N.C.H. = Actual Nursing Care Hours***

Example 8: Nursing Salary Variance Report

This report, shown in Table 8.7, is useful to nursing managers and CNOs because it demonstrates variances and the dollars associated with staffing. The actual dollars spent can then be compared to the revenue to see if revenue exceeds expenses or if expenses exceed revenue.

TABLE 8.7 NURSING SALARY VARIANCE REPORT

View YTD Template

Budget Patient Days:	161
Actual Blended Census:	171
Budget Blended Census:	160
Blended Census:	8.7

Job Code	Job Description	Prod Hours	Non Prod Hours	Actual FTE	Bud Prod Hrs	Bud Non Prod Hrs	Budget FTE	FTE Variance
1734	Nurse Manager	157.68	14.32	1.00	152.57	18.86	1.00	0.00
1744	Assistant Nurse Manager	0.00	0.00	0.00	0.00	0.00	0.00	0.00
2865	Coordinator (exempt)	0.00	0.00	0.00	0.00	0.00	0.00	0.00
3703	Unit Clerk	491.67	(15.36)	2.78	355.49	43.94	2.33	(0.45)
5050	RN, BU	2265.42	510.51	16.19	2235.20	259.51	14.55	(1.64)
5051	RN, Baylor BU	(8.51)	0.00	(0.05)	0.00	0.00	0.00	0.05
5054	RN, Per Diem BU	419.27	0.00	2.45	0.00	0.00	0.00	(2.45)
5730	Sitter (reassign from prim. Jot	36.54	0.00	0.21	0.00	0.00	0.00	(0.21)
5736	Nurse Aide	125.87	20.50	0.85	149.11	17.30	0.97	0.12
5757	Technician, Monitor	0.00	0.00	0.00	0.00	0.00	0.00	0.00
5778	Unit Coordinator--LPN	200.87	44.59	1.43	355.49	43.94	2.33	0.90
9000	Unit Clerk Re-assignment	0.00	0.00	0.00	0.00	0.00	0.00	0.00
9500	W/C Light Duty	20.72	0.00	0.12	0.00	0.00	0.00	(0.12)
0	Overtime Premium	0.00	0.00	0.00	0.00	0.00	0.00	0.00
0	Holiday 1.5x Premium	0.00	0.00	0.00	0.00	0.00	0.00	0.00
0	Shift Differential	0.00	0.00	0.00	0.00	0.00	0.00	0.00
0	On-Call	0.00	0.00	0.00	0.00	0.00	0.00	0.00
0	Special	0.00	0.00	0.00	0.00	0.00	0.00	0.00
0	LTS	0.00	0.00	0.00	0.00	0.00	0.00	0.00
0	PIP Premium	0.00	0.00	0.00	0.00	0.00	0.00	0.00
		3709.53	**574.56**	**24.99**	**3247.86**	**383.55**	**21.18**	**(3.81)**

Hours of Care per Skill Position

Job Category	Actual	Budget	Actual	Budget	Variance
RN	13.2	13.97	95,387.06	100,951.31	5564.25
RN, Per Diem BU	2.45	0	23,631.45	0.00	(23631.45)
Nursing Aide	0.74	0.93	2,323.06	2,919.52	596.46
LPN	0	0	0.00	0.00	0.00
	16.39	**14.9**	**121,341.57**	**103,870.83**	**(17470.74)**

Actual Rate	Budget Rate	Rate Diff	Actual Dollars	Budget Dollars	Rate Variance	Efficiency Variance	Total Variance
48.11	50.7	2.59	8,274.93	8,692.00	445.97	(28.90)	417.07
0.00	0.00	0.00	0.00	0.00	0.00	0.00	0.00
0.00	0.00	0.00	0.00	0.00	0.00	0.00	0.00
21.36	21.57	0.20	10,175.78	8,615.00	97.39	(1658.17)	(1560.78)
41.14	42.26	1.12	114,195.49	105,424.00	3,112.59	(11884.08)	(8771.49)
73.73	0.00	(73.73)	(627.48)	0.00	0.00	627.48	627.48
56.41	0.00	(56.41)	23,649.50	0.00	0.00	(23649.50)	(23649.50)
18.54	0.00	(18.54)	677.42	0.00	0.00	(677.42)	(677.42)
18.42	18.36	(0.06)	2,695.49	3,055.00	(8.39)	367.90	359.51
0.00	0.00	0.00	0.00	0.00	0.00	0.00	0.00
29.84	30.62	0.78	7,324.47	12,231.00	191.79	4,714.74	4,906.53
0.00	0.00	0.00	0.00	0.00	0.00	0.00	0.00
18.79	0.00	(18.79)	389.32	0.00	0.00	(389.32)	(389.32)
0.00	0.00	0.00	5,520.64	4,075.00	0.00	(1445.64)	(1445.64)
0.00	0.00	0.00	476.71	456.00	0.00	(20.71)	(20.71)
0.00	0.00	0.00	8,294.73	9,203.00	0.00	908.27	908.27
0.00	0.00	0.00	156.00	57.00	0.00	(99.00)	(99.00)
0.00	0.00	0.00	2,505.33	0.00	0.00	(2505.33)	(2505.33)
0.00	0.00	0.00	0.00	0.00	0.00	0.00	0.00
0.00	0.00	0.00	423.36	151.00	0.00	(272.36)	(272.36)
			184,131.69	**151,959.00**	**3,839.36**	**(36012.05)**	**(32172.69)**

Summary

This chapter discussed:

- Types of budget reports
- Examples of staff reports

“Knowledge is power.”

–Francis Bacon

Healthcare Reform and the Affordable Care Act

Federal and state policies that focus on healthcare reimbursement have a direct impact on how services are reimbursed in healthcare facilities. For example, if the Centers for Medicare & Medicaid Services (CMS) decides to reduce Medicare payments to hospitals by 4%, the organizations that care for Medicare patients will receive less reimbursement and may have to resort to cutting costs to gain financial stability. This is why it is so critical that, as nurses, we stay attuned to what our federal and state governments are doing when it comes to legislation that affects healthcare reimbursement.

> *"The goal of healthcare reform must be high-quality, universal coverage in a cost-effective way."*
>
> *–Bernie Sanders*

The United States has an entrepreneurial healthcare system, with a variety of products in the marketplace. However, in the US healthcare delivery system, administrative functions result in huge costs.

Compared to the US, countries with fewer varieties of insurance products tend to have much lower healthcare delivery overhead.

The US health insurance market has worked well for the insurance industry but not so well for many patients and clinicians, despite passage of the Patient Protection and Affordable Care Act (ACA) in 2010. For example, in 2024, an estimated 27 million Americans were uninsured, including 3.7 million children (Cohen et al., 2025), and those with coverage were often afraid of losing it. Although 56% of working-age adults had adequate and affordable health insurance coverage, 9% were still uninsured, 12% had experienced a gap in coverage, and 23% reported being underinsured, meaning that despite having insurance they still couldn't afford adequate access to healthcare and often delayed seeking care (Collins & Gupta, 2024). Medical debt was a problem for 44% of those reporting being underinsured (Collins & Gupta, 2024). The Commonwealth Fund survey also found that almost 30% of individuals with chronic health problems such as diabetes and heart failure skipped doses of their prescription drugs or didn't take them at all due to the cost, including a small portion of those who had health insurance for the full year (Collins & Gupta, 2024). Many medical practices lack the support that they need to provide coordinated, safe, effective, outcome-oriented, patient-centered care.

Why Reform?

Arguably—and the debate about healthcare reform did result in many arguments—the US healthcare system was broken and needed to be repaired. Essential care providers faced crushing paperwork, uncertainty regarding payment, and rising healthcare costs. Insurance bureaucracy added yet more paperwork to medical practices, which reduced their time spent with patients. Patients with no or limited coverage often went without care or delayed seeking needed care and treatment. This resulted in patients presenting to emergency departments very ill and requiring costly treatment. Healthcare outcomes in the US continued to lag behind many other countries, despite the US spending far more on care.

Two essential quality indicators of a country's healthcare system are life expectancy and infant mortality. In the 2021 World Health Organization's (WHO) assessment of countries' healthcare systems, the US ranked 71st out of 183 countries analyzed for years of healthy life expectancy at 63.9 years (WHO, 2024). The US rank in 2021 for infant mortality was 57th out of 195 countries ranked, with 5.36 infant deaths per 1,000 live births (World Population Review, 2026). Also, other countries' primary care systems ranked higher than those in the US. The most recent analysis by the Commonwealth Fund comparing the US health system's performance to nine other peer nations found the US ranking last or next to last in four of the five categories of assessment (Blumenthal et al., 2024). The US ranked second in care delivery process, which measures the elements of prevention, safety, and patient engagement (Blumenthal et al., 2024). The US continues to far exceed other nations in healthcare spending, ranking the highest at 16.5% of GDP from 1980–2023, compared to the next highest, France, at 11.9% (Blumenthal et al., 2024). Projections estimate that healthcare spending in the US will continue to climb to as high as 20% of GDP by 2033 (Keehan et al., 2025). In short, the US healthcare system would benefit from reform.

What Is an Interventional System?

The US is considered an *interventional system*. Think of an interventional system as being the opposite of a prevention system. The for-profit American healthcare system often prioritizes episodic acute care over preventive and longitudinal care due to varying levels of access to preventive or quality care driven by structural inequities, affordability, unstable insurance status, and other factors for vulnerable populations.

Life expectancy in the US has increased since 1970, from 70.8 years to approximately 79 years currently (Woolf, 2023). However, it has grown at a much slower rate as compared to other nations. While Woolf acknowledges the roles of some factors under individual control (such as diet, to some extent), he also considers psychosocial and economic factors as well as other contributors, concluding that overall the data suggests "the problem is larger and more enduring than any single health problem . . . and likely involves upstream, systemic factors capable of producing widespread effects on health" (Woolf, 2023, p. 978). Some of those factors include systemic racism and sexism, environmental and climate change factors, access to affordable and fresh food, and other social determinants of health.

Primary care providers promote health. They meet with patients to discuss diet, exercise, smoking cessation, and other healthy lifestyle behaviors. They also monitor patient cholesterol, blood pressure, heart rate, and other parameters. Then, if something is abnormal or has started to elevate—for example, the patient's cholesterol level—the provider can recommend treatments and suggest healthy behaviors to avoid costly interventions. There is a correlation between regular primary care and overall health, including healthy behaviors; however, if a significant portion of Americans don't have adequate or any access to a regular primary care provider, can't afford preventive medications or treatments, and are hindered by other socioeconomic factors, then we end up as an interventional system. Shortages of primary care providers, particularly in rural areas, are another barrier.

NOTE

Countries with better health indicators than the US usually have better primary care systems and place less emphasis on hospitals and interventional systems of care (Starfield et al., 2005).

As you learned in Chapter 2, the US has contemplated healthcare reform many times over many years. To review, Figure 9.1 briefly describes healthcare reform history in the US.

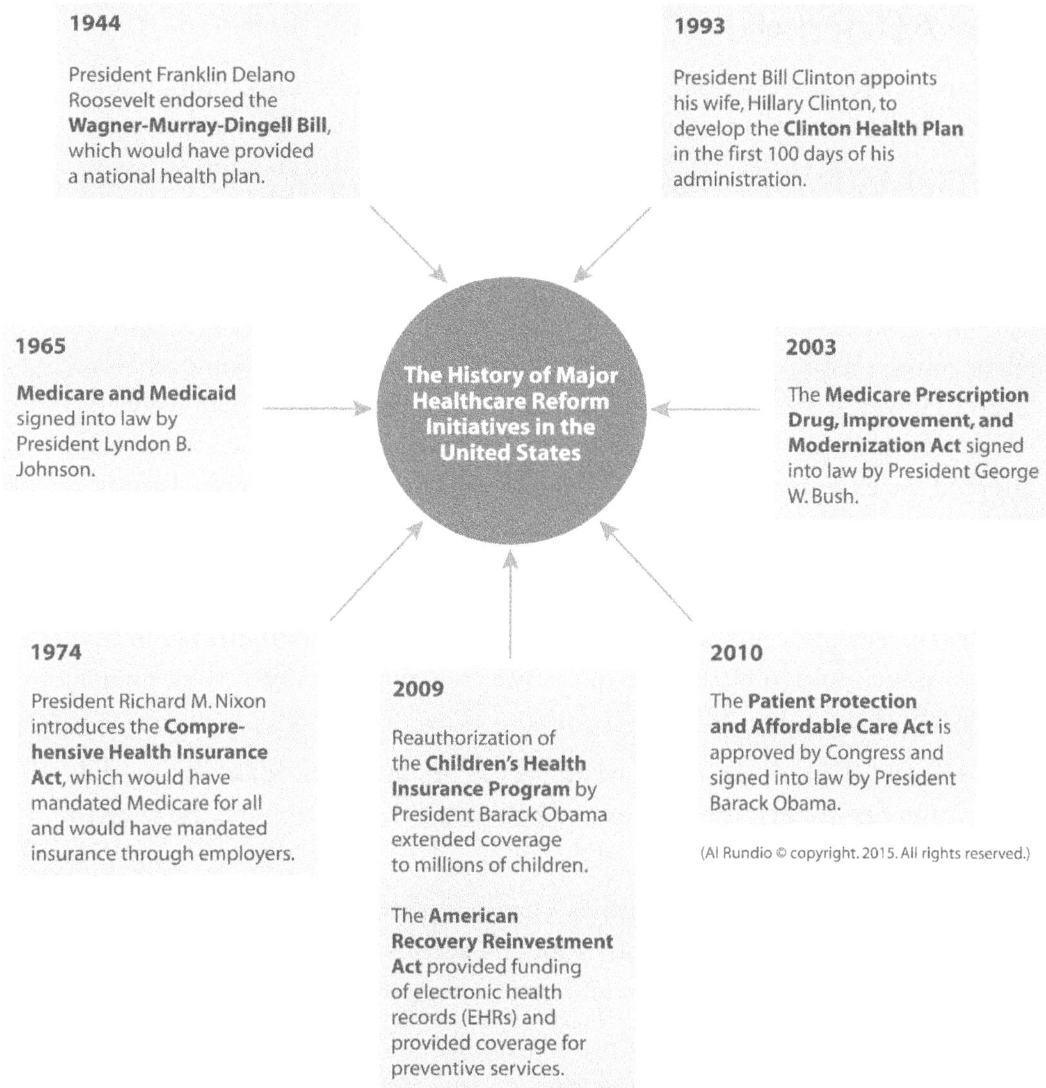

FIGURE 9.1
History of healthcare reform in the US.

The Affordable Care Act

In March 2010, the US Congress, under the Obama administration, finally passed landmark healthcare reform legislation: the Patient Protection and Affordable Care Act (ACA). This legislation was intended to address issues discussed in the previous section. In 2012, after multiple challenges at various judicial levels, the US Supreme Court ruled that the ACA was constitutional but allowed states to limit or impose conditions on coverage or even opt out of expansion entirely (Medicaid.gov, n.d.). As of early 2026, only 10 states have opted out of expanding Medicaid (Kaiser Family Foundation, 2026). However, the 2025 budget reconciliation legislation, which went into effect July 4, 2025, adds conditions and work requirements that states that adopted the expansion must implement by the end of 2026 (Kaiser Family Foundation, 2025).

The overriding themes of the ACA include:

- Increasing access to care by expanding Medicaid and insurance coverage through healthcare insurance exchanges and providing financial subsidies
- Controlling costs and making healthcare more affordable by providing tax credits, limiting out-of-pocket costs, and slowing the growth of healthcare spending
- Improving quality and health outcomes through payment reforms, care coordination, and providing incentives to providers that reward value rather than volume and award innovation
- Protecting consumers by prohibiting denial of coverage for preexisting conditions, eliminating lifetime and annual limits, and allowing young adults to remain on parents' plans until age 26
- Increasing revenue through taxes on medical devices, pharmaceutical companies, cosmetic surgery, and tanning salons, and a reduction in flexible spending accounts

- Providing financial support for nursing schools and changing loan-forgiveness programs for physicians entering the National Health Service Corps
- Emphasizing preventive care such as screenings, vaccines, and annual checkups that are covered without cost-sharing to encourage early detection and prevention
- Creating shared responsibility to individuals, employers, insurers, and the government to ensure broad participation in the healthcare system
- Reducing health disparities in healthcare access and outcomes, especially for low-income and underserved populations
- Creating more transparency between pharmaceutical companies, physicians, healthcare providers, and others
- Allowing the vast majority of young adults who are not attending college to remain on a parent's health plan until the age of 26, but coverage only applies to medical care, not dental or vision care.

New Protections

The ACA ensures fairer treatment for patients and providers. New protections eliminated insurance industry excesses and abuses in the system, such as the following:

- Denials of coverage for preexisting conditions
- Cancellation of coverage when patients make a mistake on their insurance coverage application
- Charging women more than men for similar care and procedures
- Annual and lifetime caps on benefits

In addition, before the ACA, many insurance companies spent more than 20% of every premium dollar on overhead, marketing, and chief executive officer salaries, varying by state and type of policy (Clemans-Cope, 2014).

With the passage of the ACA, insurance companies must now spend at least 80% of every premium dollar on consumer healthcare. If they do not spend this amount, they must repay the shortfall to those paying the premiums (Cotter et al., 2025).

Common Reasons for Lack of Insurance

There are various reasons for lack of insurance. Some common ones include:

- The cost of insurance is too high for some individuals.
- Many people do not have access to insurance coverage through a job, either because it's not offered or because of job loss or gaps created by job changes.
- In states that did not expand Medicaid, many individuals are ineligible for public insurance coverage.
- Illegal or undocumented immigrants are ineligible for Medicaid or marketplace insurance coverage.

(Tolbert et al., 2026)

The Patient-Centered Outcomes Research Institute (PCORI)

The PCORI is an independent, nonprofit, nongovernmental organization located in Washington, DC. The formation of this institute was authorized by Congress in 2010. The mandate of PCORI is to improve the quality and relevance of evidence available to help patients, caregivers, clinicians, employers, insurers, and policymakers make informed health decisions. This organization funds comparative clinical effectiveness research and supports work that will improve the methods used to conduct such studies. You can find more information about PCORI at http://www.pcori.org/about-us.

Figure 9.2 shows some key benefits of the ACA.

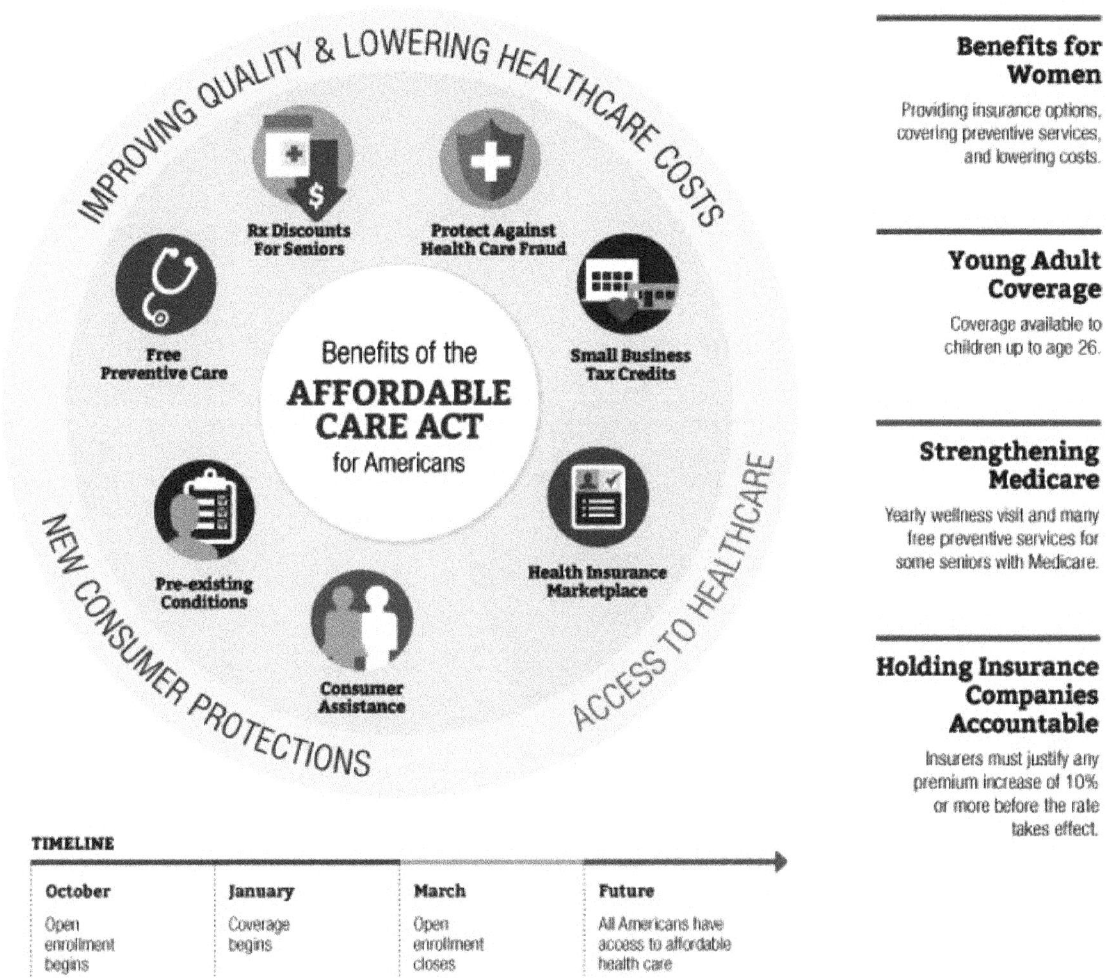

FIGURE 9.2

Benefits of the ACA (graphic from DeMichele, 2020).

NOTE

Preexisting condition insurance plans are still available. These plans are for people who have been locked out of the insurance market because of a preexisting condition such as cancer or heart disease and for reasons of cost or eligibility either choose not to or cannot participate in the marketplace plans or qualify for Medicaid or Medicare. The rules regarding these are state-specific.

Affordability

The ACA makes healthcare insurance more affordable through state health insurance exchanges, premium tax credits, and subsidies. The act also reduces the burden of uncompensated care on physicians and hospitals and provides tax credits for small businesses.

Under the ACA, the minimum essential health benefits for all persons insured in the US typically include:

- Ambulatory patient services
- Prescription pharmaceuticals
- Access to emergency services
- Inpatient hospitalization
- Maternity and newborn care
- Rehabilitative services and devices
- Laboratory services
- Mental health and substance use disorder care
- Pediatric services, including oral and vision care

The ACA also strengthened the Medicare system, preserving guaranteed benefits under Medicare, making recommended preventive services available without cost-sharing, and providing Medicare patients with an annual wellness visit. It reduced cost-sharing across the board. Finally, the ACA included strong anti-fraud measures for Medicare recipients, including tougher penalties for criminals.

Additional Benefits

Additional provisions of the ACA include:

- **Investing in training new healthcare providers and providing bonus payments to primary care providers:** This was meant to spur the addition of thousands of new doctors and nurses around the country.
- **Reducing administrative burdens:** The ACA introduced new rules to streamline, standardize, and simplify the claims and payment processes. The idea here was to reduce the number of phone calls to patients and the costs of postage and paperwork.
- **Using EHR:** The ACA called for investment in programs designed to help practices transition to electronic payment and record systems.

These provisions were geared toward enabling providers to spend more time in the exam room with patients and less time on administrative tasks.

Other benefits created by the ACA include:

- Medicare bonus payments for primary care physicians and general surgeons
- Increased Medicaid primary care payments
- Increased geographic adjustments to Medicare physician payments in 42 states and territories
- Small business tax credits for employee health insurance for many practices

Finally, the ACA built on best practices of physicians and medical groups across the country. It includes provisions for developing and implementing important payment and delivery system reforms that focus on:

- Expanding team-based care coordination
- Rewarding clinicians for care outside of traditional face-to-face visits
- Aggressively managing chronically ill patients
- Expanding access to home-based care
- Ensuring that clinicians have seamless, secure ways to share patient information and medical records

Electronic Health Records

The American Recovery and Reinvestment Act of 2009 encouraged provider investment in electronic health records (EHR). The act created financial incentives for providers who adopt EHR, which were later incorporated into the Medicare and Medicaid Promoting Interoperability Programs (PIP; CMS.gov, 2025). The Medicaid PIP ended in 2021, while the Medicare PIP continues. The program provides eligible hospitals and providers with grants to purchase, implement, and upgrade EHR systems as well as train staff in their use. To continue in the program, eligible healthcare providers and systems must meet data-reporting requirements and provide proof of "meaningful use" of the technology (American College of Physicians, 2025). By 2021, nearly 78% of private practice physician offices and almost all acute care hospitals had implemented EHR (Assistant Secretary for Technology Policy, 2022).

EHR technology promotes better-coordinated and more efficient care by:

- Reducing medical errors
- Reducing redundant testing procedures

- Having better availability of records and data
- Improving clinical decision support systems for providers
- Improving safety and convenience of electronic prescribing

This results in safer and higher quality patient care. For example, electronic prescribing eliminates handwritten prescriptions, which are often illegible; this improves safety and quality. And easier secure access to the patient's medical history assists providers in making better treatment decisions.

Accountable Care Organizations

Accountable care organizations (ACOs) are a significant concept in the ACA. ACOs create partnerships for patients—groups of doctors, hospitals, and other healthcare professionals work together to give patients high-quality, coordinated service and healthcare; improve health outcomes; and manage costs. ACOs may be in a specific geographic area and/or focused on patients who have a specific condition.

Value-based purchasing (VBP) is a critical component of an ACO. VBP is a strategy to measure, report, and reward quality and excellence in healthcare delivery. Hospital VBP is part of the CMS strategy to link Medicare's payment system to a value-based system. This system rewards hospitals that improve healthcare quality; it focuses on quality, provider performance, and patient experience (CMS, 2024).

ACOs consist of many types of providers, including:

- Primary care providers
- Acute care providers
- Psychiatric/mental healthcare providers
- Rehabilitation care providers
- Home care providers

Through ACOs:

- New models of care and payment systems to support Medicare and Medicaid enrollees have been explored.
- New models of care that incorporate behavioral health into the primary care setting have been attempted.
- Comprehensive primary care initiatives and federally qualified health centers with advanced primary care practice demonstration projects have been initiated.
- Healthcare innovation challenges and programs to look at innovative models of care delivery have been implemented.

Challenges to the ACA

The ACA has undergone several changes since its inception in 2010. These include the American Rescue Plan Act (ARPA) of 2021 which, following the COVID-19 pandemic, temporarily lowered premiums and expanded affordability for many marketplace enrollees. These enhancements were extended through 2025 by the Inflation Reduction Act of 2022 but expired at the end of 2025, when Congress failed to pass an extension. The following sections outline changes that have been made to the ACA since its passage.

The Elimination of the Individual Mandate

Perhaps the most significant change made to the ACA was the elimination of the individual mandate. The *individual mandate* required people lacking health insurance coverage from their employer or some other source, as well as those who did not qualify for Medicaid or Medicare, to obtain insurance coverage—usually through an ACA insurance exchange. Under the individual mandate, anyone who did not obtain healthcare insurance faced a tax penalty. However, lawmakers revised the individual mandate to lower the tax penalty to $0 (Lasky, 2025). This effectively eliminated the mandate.

Four states have their own individual mandate that includes penalties for non-compliance: California, Massachusetts, New Jersey, and Rhode Island. Washington, DC, also has an individual mandate. Vermont has an individual mandate; however, there is no penalty for failing to comply with this mandate. In states and districts that penalize for non-compliance, individuals can seek an exemption from the penalty. (Details vary by state.) If an exemption is not granted, the penalty is applied when the individual files their state tax return (Nania & Bunis, 2024).

One State's Version of the ACA

New Jersey is one state that built its own insurance exchange to enact the provisions of the ACA. This exchange offers three primary insurance programs, including New Jersey Family Care, which includes the State Health Insurance Program for Children. Out-of-network insurance programs are also available.

The goal of the state is to have every person covered with a base level insurance plan. The state offers tax credits to lower insurance premium payments, based on an individual's level of income and the number of dependents.

Individuals can apply online through the state's insurance market website. This website also offers access to certified agents and assistants to help individuals navigate the information and programs available from this site.

The Addition of a Work Requirement for Medicaid

The ACA permitted states to expand their Medicaid programs to include all low-income adults. In addition, through the ACA Medicaid expansion provision, the income threshold was raised, thereby increasing the number of people eligible for Medicaid via the ACA. Legislative actions at the state level continued to expand Medicaid under ACA provisions, with North Carolina joining in 2023, bringing the total to 40 states plus Washington, DC (American Hospital Association, 2023). After the passage of the ACA, however, changes were made to this part of the law to allow states to require individuals to demonstrate that they were either working or attending school to be eligible for Medicaid.

The Termination of ACA Cost-Sharing Subsidies to Insurers

One key feature of the ACA was the cost-sharing reduction (CSR) subsidy, funded by the federal government. These payments reimbursed insurers for providing CSRs to eligible enrollees, helping keep premiums affordable and encouraging insurer participation in the exchanges. In October 2017, the Trump administration abruptly ended these payments, citing a lack of congressional appropriation (Wager & Cox, 2025). As a result, insurers significantly increased premiums on "silver" plans, a practice known as "silver loading," to offset the loss of funding (Wager & Cox, 2025). In January 2025, the Biden administration issued a notice codifying the practice, within certain parameters (Wager & Cox, 2025). Rather than saving the government money, however, the elimination of the original CSR subsidy has increased the federal share and contributes to the federal deficit (Wager & Cox, 2025).

The Return of "Skinny" Insurance Plans

With the enactment of the ACA, health insurance policies had to offer minimum levels of coverage. The ACA mandate required that short-term policies with less coverage—called "skinny" policies—could be used by a consumer for only three months. They were originally intended as a bridge for consumers in between health insurance coverage due to job loss or changing employers. In 2018 lawmakers changed this timeline to allow consumers to hold skinny policies for up to three years (Nania & Bunis, 2024). Consumer advocates lobbied for change, calling the policies misleading and noting they were "particularly problematic for older adults" who would not actually be covered at the advertised price since they usually have preexisting conditions. Thus, consumers would purchase the plans without realizing they actually cost more and cover less than the conventional marketplace plans. Beginning in 2023, the departments of Health and Human Services, Labor, and Treasury jointly applied a new rule limiting the policies to three months again and only an additional month as a possible extension (Nania & Bunis, 2024).

NOTE

Many efforts to change or even repeal the ACA have occurred since its passage. Not only can the president of the US request changes to the ACA, but whichever political party is in control of both the House of Representatives and the Senate can, too.

Premium Tax Credits and Cost-Sharing Subsidies to Consumers

Enhanced premium tax credits and cost-sharing subsidies direct to consumers were introduced in the ACA upon implementation and were expanded in 2021 through the ARPA as part of the COVID-19 relief legislation (Singh, 2024) and set to expire at the end of 2025. Congress did not pass an extension, so these tax credits and subsidies are now gone. Premium costs for ACA plans have risen sharply as a result, as much as doubling for the 93% of Americans who were receiving premium tax credits under ARPA (Lukens & Zhang, 2025). Early reporting shows the loss of the tax credit and subsidies has already resulted in 10% of those previously enrolled in marketplace plans now being uninsured (Lopes et al., 2026), with future estimates of around 4 million people losing coverage due to cost (Blavin & Simpson, 2025; Economic Security Project Action, 2025; Shaw, 2025).

The expiration of these subsidies will impact healthcare providers directly with a loss of an estimated $32 billion just in 2026 due to the consequent reduction in healthcare spending and an estimated increase of $7.7 billion in the demand for uncompensated care (Blavin & Simpson, 2025). Rural hospitals are expected to be hardest hit, with some estimating that "at least 300 rural hospitals are at risk of closing in the next 2–3 years" (Economic Security Project Action, 2025, p. 1).

Changes to Eligibility and Cost-Sharing Requirements

The 2025 Budget Reconciliation Act (P.L. 119-21) introduced significant changes to Medicaid and ACA-related provisions. Key elements include (Congressional Research Service, 2025):

- **Medicaid work requirements:** For the first time, the federal government is mandating that states require certain adults (primarily those in the ACA expansion group) to meet "community engagement" requirements—such as work, job training, or volunteering—to maintain eligibility. These requirements are mandatory and cannot be waived, with implementation deadlines starting in late 2026.
- **Eligibility restrictions:** The law tightens eligibility by requiring more frequent renewals (every six months instead of annually) and limiting immigration statuses eligible for Medicaid (excluding refugees and asylum seekers, for example). It also eliminates financial incentives for states to expand Medicaid under the ACA.
- **Cost-sharing requirements:** States must impose new copayments (up to $35 per service) for certain Medicaid expansions for adults, excluding primary care, mental health, and substance use disorder services.

Ongoing debate and legislative actions continue to reform the ACA's structure and cost-sharing requirements, the full impact of which remains to be seen. It is important for nurse managers to stay abreast of changes that will impact the overall operation of their units and the organization. These are changing rapidly and often!

Hospital Mergers, Closures, and Strategic Partnering

In many states, hospitals have begun to merge into larger health systems, resulting in the subsequent closure of some hospitals. Anecdotally, many doubt that a single hospital will survive in the near future. Some predict that there will instead be 100 to 200 large regional health systems. Others predict fewer larger national health systems; instead, for example, every hospital will be part of one of eight or 10 national systems, with a few independent hospitals surviving as stand-alone facilities.

Let's consider the state where I vacation as a microcosm of what may occur. New Jersey is a very densely populated state that encompasses both urban and rural environments. It is sandwiched in the northeast corridor with easy access to major cities like Philadelphia, New York, Baltimore, Boston, and Washington, DC. It is located in one of the busiest areas in the country, so I believe that it is a good representation of what may come in the future.

New Jersey is seeing mergers in healthcare systems (for example, two hospital systems coming together as one, or smaller health systems with three or four hospitals), with some stand-alone hospitals still surviving. Almost all these types of delivery systems now engage in what is known as *strategic partnering*. Strategic partnering involves partnering with other types of facilities—not necessarily healthcare facilities—to achieve economies of scale and to maximize talent. One example is a hospital system partnering with a university. Certain services, like dietary services, could be shared between both organizations. The university could bring additional talent to the hospital system, and the hospital could serve as the major clinical site for the education of physicians, nurses, and other healthcare providers.

Another trend is that hospitals and hospital systems are moving beyond the walls of the hospital to focus on population health. For example, one health system has more than 60 outpatient facilities in various communities. These facilities include:

- Urgent care centers
- Convenient care centers in places like shopping centers, stores, and pharmacies
- Health and wellness centers
- Radiology and laboratory centers
- Home health agencies

There is a new push toward *site neutrality*. This is a healthcare payment policy approach where Medicare pays the same amount for the same service regardless of whether it is provided in a hospital outpatient department, an independent physician office, or an ambulatory surgical center. The goal is to curb costs by reducing the higher reimbursement rates hospitals receive for outpatient services and to curb hospital consolidation by eliminating the incentive to buy physician practices. Proponents argue that it would lower patient costs and foster competition, while opponents, like the American Hospital Association, claim it would decrease patient access to critical services, especially in rural areas (American Hospital Association, 2025). This can make it difficult for health systems to open new access points due to the decreased reimbursements.

The reality is that healthcare and healthcare delivery systems are changing, and changing reimbursement and finance is one of the major catalysts for this change. Nurse managers and future nurse managers need to be aware of this changing financial landscape so you can be better prepared to develop, implement, and monitor budgets; allocate resources to your staff; and ensure quality patient care with excellent outcomes. Nurses and nurse managers are in a position to be key partners and change agents in an evolving healthcare delivery system.

The Future of Healthcare?

While the ACA continues to face challenges from some political sectors, most agree we must do better in reducing healthcare spending and improving affordability for consumers. Therefore, there are other proposals to expand or replace the current version of the ACA. Two of these proposals are different types of global caps and Medicare for All.

Price Caps and Price Setting

In 2012, lawmakers in Massachusetts proposed legislation that would establish a global cap on healthcare costs (Kliff, 2012). The Massachusetts healthcare system, signed into law in 2006 by then-governor Mitt Romney, served as a model for the ACA. Such global caps can be applied in a variety of ways. Overall, the idea is to use regulatory approaches to constrain healthcare spending since competition and market-based policies have not worked. Most of these proposals focus on providers, hospitals, insurance companies, and other third-party payers rather than individuals. With this approach, the cost of healthcare expenditures is averaged across an entire facility or roster of patients; this average then defines the cap. Some of these cost-saving caps include:

- Price regulation
    - **Price setting:** Sets a fixed price for each service, such as is currently used in the Medicare Physician Fee Schedule; if the price is set too low, it could affect providers' bottom line and reduce access and quality of care.
    - **Price caps:** Sets a maximum price for a service, similar to the Montana State Employee Health Plan (Pany et al., 2022); finding the right price balance is key since setting it too high would have little positive effect and setting it too low would negatively affect the providers and consumers in the same way as price setting.

- **Price growth caps:** Imposes a limit on how much prices can be increased over a specific period of time, similar to the Rhode Island Affordability Standards (Pany et al., 2022); while this would not immediately reduce spending, it would limit it in the long term.

- **Global budgets:** These policies limit spending for a specific patient population over a specific period of time, such as the Maryland All-Payer Model (Pany et al., 2022); vulnerable to changes in the patient volume or other factors that could occur during the specified time period resulting in providers being under-compensated.
- **Spending growth targets:** This approach limits overall healthcare expenditure increases, similar to the Massachusetts Health Care Cost Growth Benchmark (Pany et al., 2022); these may be mandatory or voluntary and are usually set annually and monitored by an independent government agency.

Some believe that global caps will help to control healthcare costs. Others think that some patients will not obtain treatments they need because hospitals and insurance companies will deny some services to stay within the global capped amount. Still others argue that until consumers become more involved and accountable for their health, healthcare costs will continue to be difficult to control, caps or no.

NOTE

Capitation is a precursor to global caps, and some consider it a form of global caps. With capitation, one fee per member per month is paid to the provider, regardless of how often an individual member accesses (or doesn't access) health services.

Medicare for All

Legislation calling for some form of universal healthcare coverage in the US has repeatedly been introduced in Congress. The most recent proposal is called Medicare for All, spearheaded by US Representatives Pramila Jayapal (D-WA) and Debbie Dingell (D-MI) and US Senator Bernie Sanders (I-VT), who introduced the Medicare for All Act in April of 2025. Polling shows as many as 62% of Americans believe the government should provide healthcare coverage for everyone (Jones, 2024). Under the terms of the proposal, Medicare would be expanded to provide comprehensive health, dental, hearing, and vision care to every American without premiums, co-payments, or deductibles. Consumers would be able to freely choose their care providers without needing to fill out paperwork or seek approval ("Jayapal," 2025).

While estimates in cost savings if enacted vary widely, one Congressional Budget Office analysis stated that a single-payer healthcare system most similar to the current Medicare for All proposal would reduce healthcare costs by $300 to $650 billion by 2030 (Bruenig, 2020). Opponents say the projected savings are misleading because they do not account for how the program would be funded (Merkley, 2022). However, proponents state that the program will be funded through increased income taxes on the wealthiest. They also point out the many peer countries with decades of successful single-payer healthcare systems. Supporters of Medicare for All include healthcare organizations such as National Nurses United, Physicians for a National Health Program, American Medical Student Association, National Union of Healthcare Workers, and the American Public Health Association ("Jayapal," 2025).

One would need a crystal ball to predict what will occur next in healthcare. What is for certain is that the focus on controlling and reducing costs, while simultaneously improving quality and outcomes, is here to stay.

Summary

This chapter discussed:

- The need for healthcare reform
- The Affordable Care Act
- Challenges to the Affordable Care Act
- Hospital mergers, closures, and strategic partnering
- Global caps and price setting
- Medicare for All proposals

> *"Of all the forms of inequality, injustice in healthcare is the most inhumane."*
>
> *–Martin Luther King, Jr.*

References

American College of Physicians. (2025). *Medicare and Medicaid incentive programs.* https://www.acponline.org/medicare-and-medicaid-incentive-programs#:~:text=The%20CMS%20Electronic%20Health%20Record,use%22%20of%20certified%20EHR%20technology

American Hospital Association. (2023, Dec. 1). *North Carolina becomes 40th state to expand Medicaid under the ACA.* https://www.aha.org/news/headline/2023-12-01-north-carolina-becomes-40th-state-expand-medicaid-under-aca

American Hospital Association. (2025, May). *Fact sheet: Medicare site-neutral legislative proposals under consideration would jeopardize access to care for patients and communities.* https://www.aha.org/system/files/media/file/2025/05/fact-sheet-medicare-site-neutral-legislative-proposals-under-consideration-would-jeopardize-access-to-care-for-patients-and-communities.pdf

Assistant Secretary for Technology Policy. (2022, March). *National trends in hospital and physician adoption of electronic health records.* Health IT Research & Analysis. https://healthit.gov/data/quickstats/national-trends-hospital-and-physician-adoption-electronic-health-records/#:~:text=End%20of%20interactive%20chart.,physicians%20had%20adopted%20an%20EHR

Blavin, F., & Simpson, M. (2025, September). *Changes in health care spending and uncompensated care under Enhanced Tax Credit expiration for Marketplace coverage: Updated 2026 state and national estimates.* Urban Institute. https://www.urban.org/research/publication/changes-health-care-spending-and-uncompensated-care-under-enhanced-tax-credit

Blumenthal, D., Gumas, E. D., Shah, A., Gunja, M. Z., & Williams, R. D., II. (2024, Sept. 19). *Mirror, mirror 2024: A portrait of the failing US health system.* The Commonwealth Fund. https://www.commonwealthfund.org/publications/fund-reports/2024/sep/mirror-mirror-2024

Bruenig, M. (2020, Dec. 11). *CBO: Medicare for All reduces health spending.* People's Policy Project. https://www.peoplespolicyproject.org/2020/12/11/cbo-medicare-for-all-reduces-health-spending/

Centers for Medicare & Medicaid Services. (2024). *The hospital value-based purchasing (VBP) program.* https://www.cms.gov/Medicare/Quality-Initiatives-Patient-Assessment-Instruments/Value-Based-Programs/HVBP/Hospital-Value-Based-Purchasing

Clemans-Cope, L. (2014, Jan. 3). *The ACA's 80/20 rule could lead to higher value health insurance in some states.* Urban Institute. https://www.urban.org/urban-wire/acas-8020-rule-could-lead-higher-value-health-insurance-some-states

CMS.gov. (2025, Nov. 24). *Promoting interoperability programs.* https://www.cms.gov/medicare/regulations-guidance/promoting-interoperability-programs?redirect=/ehrincentiveprograms/

Cohen, R. A., Briones, E. M., & Sohi, I. (2025, June 20). *Health insurance coverage: Early release of estimates from the National Health Interview Survey, 2024.* National Center for Health Statistics. https://www.cdc.gov/nchs/data/nhis/earlyrelease/insur202506.pdf

Collins, S. R., & Gupta, A. (2024, November). *The state of health insurance coverage in the US: Findings from the Commonwealth Fund 2024 Biennial Health Insurance Survey.* The Commonwealth Fund. https://doi.org/10.26099/byce-qc28

Congressional Research Service. (2025, Aug. 18). *Health provisions in P.L. 119-21, the FY2025 Reconciliation Law* (CRS Report R48633). https://www.congress.gov/crs-product/R48633

Cotter, L., Rae, M., McGough, M., Rakshit, S., & Cox, C. (2025, Nov. 3). *How ACA Marketplace costs compare to employer-sponsored health insurance.* Peterson-KFF Health System Tracker. https://www.healthsystemtracker.org/brief/how-aca-marketplace-costs-compare-to-employer-sponsored-health-insurance/#Comparison%20of%20individual%20and%20group%20monthly%20premium%20and%20claim%20utilization,%202024

DeMichele, T. (2020, Sept. 2). *Benefits of ObamaCare: Advantage of ObamaCare.* https://obamacarefacts.com/benefitsofobamacare/

Economic Security Policy Action. (2025). *Timeline of impacts—American healthcare.* https://economicsecurity.us/wp-content/uploads/2025/10/Healthcare-Timeline-of-Impacts-from-H.R.1.pdf

"Jayapal, Sanders, Diongell, hundreds of health care workers introduce Medicare for All." (2025, April 29). [Press release.] https://jayapal.house.gov/2025/04/29/jayapal-sanders-dingell-hundreds-of-health-care-workers-introduce-medicare-for-all/

Jones, J. (2024, Dec. 9). *More in US see health coverage as government responsibility.* Gallup. https://news.gallup.com/poll/654101/health-coverage-government-responsibility.aspx#:~:text=Public%20opinion%20shifted%20back%20to,and%202007%2C%20expressed%20that%20opinion

Kaiser Family Foundation. (2025, July 8). *Health provisions in the 2025 federal budget reconciliation bill.* https://www.kff.org/medicaid/tracking-the-medicaid-provisions-in-the-2025-budget-bill/

Kaiser Family Foundation. (2026, March 12). *Status of state Medicaid expansion decisions.* https://www.kff.org/medicaid/status-of-state-medicaid-expansion-decisions/#:~:text=In%20July%202025%2C%20Governor%20Mike,)%20is%20reduced%20below%2090%25

Keehan, S. P., Madison, A. J., Poisal, J. A., Cuckler, G. A., Smith, S. D., Sisko, A. M., Fiore, J. A., & Rennie, K. E. (2025, June 25). National health expenditure projections, 2024–2033: Despite insurance coverage declines, health to grow as share of GDP. *Health Affairs, 44*(7). https://doi.org/10.1377/hlthaff.2025.00545

Kliff, S. (2012, July 31). Massachusetts aims for another health care first: A global spending cap. *The Washington Post.* https://www.washingtonpost.com/news/wonk/wp/2012/07/31/massachusetts-aims-for-another-health-care-first-a-global-spending-cap/

Lasky, J. (2025). *Constitutional challenges to the Affordable Care Act*. EBSCO Research Starters. https://www.ebsco.com/research-starters/consumer-health/constitutional-challenges-affordable-care-act

Lopes, L., Valdes, I., Sparks, G., Mulugeta, M., & Kirzinger, A. (2026, March 19). *Cost concerns and coverage changes: A follow-up survey of ACA Marketplace enrollees*. Kaiser Family Foundation. https://www.kff.org/public-opinion/a-follow-up-survey-of-aca-marketplace-enrollees/

Lukens, G., & Zhang, E. (2025, Nov. 3). *Health insurance premium spikes imminent as tax credit enhancements set to expire*. Center on Budget & Policy Priorities. https://www.cbpp.org/research/health/health-insurance-premium-spikes-imminent-as-tax-credit-enhancements-set-to-expire

Medicaid.gov. (n.d.). *Eligibility policy*. https://www.medicaid.gov/medicaid/eligibility-policy

Merkley, J. (2022, May 12). *Correct the record: "Medicare for All" means Medicare for none*. US Senate Committee on the Budget [Press release]. https://www.budget.senate.gov/ranking-member/newsroom/press/correct-the-record-medicare-for-all-means-medicare-for-none

Nania, R., & Bunis, D. (2024, March 29). *New federal rule curbs short-term insurance plans*. AARP. https://www.aarp.org/health/healthcare/federal-goverment-rule-short-term-insurance-plans/

Pany, M., Biniek, J. F., & Neuman, T. (2022, May 31). *Price regulation, global budgets, and spending targets: A road map to reduce health care spending, and improve affordability*. Kaiser Family Foundation. https://www.kff.org/health-costs/price-regulation-global-budgets-and-spending-targets-a-road-map-to-reduce-health-care-spending-and-improve-affordability/

Shaw, T. (2025, Nov. 4). *Estimated impact of ACA premium tax credit expiration*. Thomson Reuters. https://tax.thomsonreuters.com/news/estimated-impact-of-aca-premium-tax-credit-expiration/

Singh, R. (2024, Oct. 1). *A brief history of the Affordable Care Act*. Kaiser Family Foundation. https://www.kff.org/quick-take/a-brief-history-of-the-affordable-care-act/

Starfield, B., Shi, L., & Macinko, J. (2005). Contribution of primary care to health systems and health. *The Milbank Quarterly, 83*(3), 457–502. https://doi.org/10.1111/j.1468-0009.2005.00409.x

Tolbert, J., Cervantes, S., Bell, C., & Damico, A. (2026, April 9). *Key facts about the uninsured population.* Kaiser Family Foundation. https://www.kff.org/uninsured/key-facts-about-the-uninsured-population/

Wager, E., & Cox, C. (2025, June 26). *Explaining cost-sharing reductions and silver loading in ACA marketplaces.* Kaiser Family Foundation. https://www.kff.org/affordable-care-act/explaining-cost-sharing-reductions-and-silver-loading-in-aca-marketplaces/

Woolf, S. H. (2023). Falling behind: The growing gap in life expectancy between the United States and other countries, 1933–2021. *American Journal of Public Health, 113*(9), 929–1032. https://doi.org/10.2105/AJPH.2023.307310

World Health Organization. (2024). *WHO global progress dashboard: Healthy life expectancy (HALE).* https://data.who.int/dashboards/global-progress

World Population Review. (2026). *Infant mortality rate by country 2026.* https://worldpopulationreview.com/country-rankings/infant-mortality-rate-by-country

Governing Boards of Healthcare Organizations and Specialty Nursing Organizations

A book on budgeting and finance in healthcare isn't really complete without a discussion of governing boards and specialty organizations. This chapter discusses both of these topics. But first, let's make the case for why nurses should serve on boards:

- Nurses are the largest workforce in healthcare but represent less than 5% of all health system board seats, per a 2022 survey (American Hospital Association, 2026).

> "Serving others prepares you to lead others."
>
> –Jim George

- Nurses can contribute a clinical and operational voice in the boardroom that is often missing.
- Nurses serving on a health system or hospital board is an opportunity to benefit both the consumers of healthcare and the nursing workforce.
- Nurses can also contribute to a variety of nonprofit and for-profit boards to impact and improve the health of the communities they serve.

Regardless of the type of organization, there are fundamental responsibilities and characteristics of boards that their members must consider.

The Four Duties of a Board

- **Duty of care:** Each board member has a legal responsibility to participate actively in making decisions on behalf of the organization and to exercise their best judgment while doing so.
- **Duty of loyalty:** Each board member must put the interests of the organization before their personal and professional interests when acting on behalf of the organization in a decision-making capacity. The organization's needs come first.
- **Duty of obedience:** Board members bear the legal responsibility of ensuring that the organization complies with the applicable federal, state, and local laws and adheres to its mission.
- **Duty of oversight:** Board members are required to make a good-faith effort to ensure that the organization has implemented proper reporting systems and appropriately address "red flags" suggestive of corporate wrongdoing.

Characteristics of High-Performing Boards

- **Strategic:** Avoids delving into minutia; understands governance
- **Accountable:** Follows through on commitments and promises
- **Respected:** Has the esteem of the community
- **Respectful:** Demonstrates respect toward all persons; expresses gratitude and shares credit with others
- **Team-oriented:** Understands and practices collaboration
- **Innovative:** Uses ingenuity and resources to solve problems
- **Confidential:** Treats discussions and documents with discretion
- **Performance-based:** Sets metrics and expects results
- **Grateful:** Says thank-you and recognizes the accomplishments of others

What Is a Governing Board?

The purpose of an organization's governing body is just as its name implies: governance. More specifically, governing boards, though they vary by individual bylaws, are responsible for financial stewardship and organizational strategy, including quality, safety, enterprise risk, compliance, CEO evaluation, mission, and community accountability.

The governing body for a hospital or healthcare system typically consists of:

- A board of directors
- The chief executive officer, or CEO (although this may not be a voting member of the board in some organizations)
- Nonvoting members, such as the chief nursing officer (CNO) or chief financial officer (CFO), who may or may not routinely attend all board meetings

While this is the general structure, nonprofit vs. for-profit structures and bylaws regarding the members of the board and their levels of participation vary.

Governing bodies also generally have an executive committee. For example, on a hospital board, the executive committee might consist of:

- Chair
- First vice chair
- Second vice chair
- Treasurer
- Secretary

NOTE

Titles as well as term limits vary from organization to organization. These are regulated by board bylaws.

Governing boards for hospitals and healthcare systems are typically broken down into committees such as strategic planning, quality and safety, and finance. In addition, ad hoc committees may be appointed to study special issues or circumstances and report back to the board. When the work of the ad hoc committee has been completed, the committee is dissolved.

Health System Network Boards Versus Health System Hospital Boards: What's the Difference?

Simply stated, the major difference between a health system network board and a health system hospital board is that the network board focuses on broad organizational issues across the entire healthcare system and the communities within that system, while the hospital board focuses on issues pertaining to a specific hospital(s) within the system and the communities that hospital(s) serves. As an example, consider quality improvement. A network board focuses on quality throughout the entire system, while a hospital board focuses on quality indicators in that specific hospital.

The Responsibilities of a Governing Board

Governing board members have a critical fiduciary responsibility. They provide financial oversight to ensure that the organization remains fiscally sound and play a major role in determining how funds are spent.

Other primary responsibilities of a governing board for a hospital or healthcare system typically are:

- Hiring and evaluating the CEO to manage and run day-to-day operations at the facility
- Ensuring fiscal accountability
- Giving final approval on all policies and procedures
- Credentialing the medical and associate medical staff—for example, advanced practice nurses
- Ensuring quality and safety
- Strategic planning
- Handling capital improvement projects
- Fundraising
- Engaging in community activism
- Making major human capital resources decisions (that is, what employees contribute dollar-wise to their health benefits)

NOTE

The primary role of a governing body is oversight, not day-to-day operational management.

As mentioned, a key focus of governing boards for hospitals and health systems is ensuring quality and patient safety. In fact, quality improvement is now *the* number-one focus of these boards. Quality should be the primary mission of any healthcare facility! Finance is one driving force behind the effort to improve quality. To maximize reimbursement and ensure evidence-based care, quality metrics must be met.

NOTE

High-reliability healthcare organizations strive for zero events—that is, events that should never occur, such as wrong-site surgeries. These organizations are on a quest for quality every day.

Healthcare facilities with the best quality outcomes are those in which quality starts at the top—with the board and the CEO, who breathe quality into the culture. In their pursuit of quality, these governing boards also:

- Regularly review metrics using a dashboard or scorecard
- Review all sentinel events—that is, unexpected occurrences that cause death, permanent harm, or severe temporary harm, and/or events requiring intervention to sustain life
- Create incentive programs for providers
- Ensure evidence-informed decision-making
- Encourage input from multiple stakeholders
- Use continuous measurement with good feedback loops
- Engage patients

NOTE

Transparency and accountability are key to quality.

Conflicts of Interest

A *conflict of interest* is any situation where personal interests could influence—or appear to influence—official decisions. In the case of a conflict of interest, a person likely gains something (usually financial in nature). With many conflicts of interest, legal and ethical issues come into play.

Here's an example. Suppose I own a company that supplies a certain healthcare-related product, and I become a board member for a hospital that uses that same product. This represents a potential conflict of interest because I could be perceived as reaping a financial benefit by serving on the hospital board.

Here's another example. Suppose John owned a real estate company. A local hospital, which occasionally purchases nearby properties for the purposes of expansion, invited John to join its board, believing John's real estate expertise would be useful for these types of transactions. John accepted. Soon thereafter, with John acting as the realtor, the hospital purchased a nearby parcel of land for the future development of a long-term care facility. Later, however, the hospital learned that John had secretly purchased the land beforehand and then sold it to the hospital for a highly inflated price. This represents an ethical and legal lapse on John's part. Although John did serve the hospital's interests by helping it obtain the land it wanted, he padded his own pockets in the process. Moreover, by overcharging the hospital for the land, John limited the amount of money the hospital could spend on the new care facility. The hospital eventually terminated John. Of course, there was nothing wrong with asking a real estate agent to serve on the board, but when it came time to purchase property, it would have been more ethical to employ an outside agency.

NOTE

Members of a governing board must be honest, ethical, forthright, and objective.

Tips to Avoid Conflicts of Interest

Here are a few tips to help you avoid conflicts of interest:

- **Disclosure:** When in doubt, disclose potential conflicts of interest.
- **Avoidance:** Avoid situations in which you might personally benefit (especially financially).
- **Transparency:** Be transparent and honest in all interactions.
- **Moral compass:** Know your own ethical values and moral compass and have the moral courage to do what is right.
- **Consultation:** When in doubt as to whether a conflict exists, consult an attorney who can advise you accordingly.
- **Your moral gut:** This is what I feel is perhaps most important. If your gut tells you that something just doesn't seem right, then avoid it. Your gut is usually correct!

Corporate Compliance Committees

Many governing boards include a *corporate compliance committee*, sometimes called an *ethics and audit committee*. The primary purpose of this committee is to ensure the organization complies with laws, rules, ethics, and regulations, and that no conflicts of interest exist.

The corporate compliance committee normally conducts a number of audits per year to assess whether compliance in all areas is being met. Employees who serve on the committee also educate staff throughout the organization in an effort to ensure compliance.

Non-compliance in key areas, especially violations of federal laws, can be very costly to an organization. For example, a HIPAA or EMTALA violation can not only result in heavy fines but also impact an organization's reputation.

Interview With a Corporate Compliance Committee Vice President

Q. *What are some of your responsibilities?*

A. One of the major responsibilities that I have is to make certain that the committee has a well-thought-out plan.

Q. *How do you develop your plan?*

A. Our organization contracts with an outside consultant to assist us with a road map, so to speak, on how to structure the key elements of the corporate compliance program. The organization entertained competitive bids from outside vendors. We then had a subcommittee review six vendors, and two were recommended to the board. Once selected, this consulting firm interviewed the board members with a series of questions that ascertained key information for focusing the committee's work. Based on this information, the consulting firm then made recommendations for the six audits that we will conduct this year. The consulting firm assists us with the plan for each audit, the timeline, and reports. They then meet with the committee periodically to review progress as well as any issues. We have found that this has greatly improved compliance in our organization.

Q. *What is a typical committee meeting like?*

A. Our committee meets quarterly. At these meetings, my staff and I present key metrics from audits, educational events, and other activities. Our hospital lawyer also attends these meetings. He provides a report of any pending legal issues regarding compliance in the organization. He also reports on any changes in law pertaining to compliance happening at a national level. This keeps our board members informed as well as educated.

Common Mistakes With Governing Boards

There are a few common mistakes that governing boards make that reduce their effectiveness. These include:

- **Lack of term limits or term limits that are too long:** Hospital boards have generally concluded that it is best to implement term limits—preferably short ones, but the specifics vary widely. Some term limits don't allow consecutive terms of service or require a "cooling off" period before a member can serve again.
- **No rotation of the chairperson:** Rotating board leadership—especially the chairperson—allows the organization to generate new ideas and gain new perspective. Having a different chair can breathe new life into an organization.
- **Too many board members:** The larger the board, the more difficult it becomes to make decisions, and the less likely it is that all board members will read and complete all the preparatory work that is necessary to serve on a board.
- **Too few board members:** The main issue here is that there might not be enough members to have quorum for voting if certain members miss board meetings.
- **Lack of commitment of board members:** Being a board member takes time—not just during the meetings but beforehand, to prepare. Members who lack commitment often fail to do the necessary prep work, meaning they cannot effectively contribute during board meetings. This is often especially true among board members for not-for-profit organizations, who usually serve on a voluntary basis.

- **Unfamiliarity with the primary purpose of the organization:** Healthcare is much different from organizations that board members might work for or own. It is often difficult for some board members to grasp the primary purpose of the healthcare organization. It is also difficult for these board members to understand the complex billing, coding, and financial systems of healthcare.

NOTE

Good boards conduct periodic self-evaluations to assess their effectiveness.

The Role of Nurses on Governing Boards

Many boards lack authorities on quality, safety, and the patient experience. Enter nurses. Nurses can be extremely valuable contributors to the governing board of any hospital or other healthcare organization. They bring many positive attributes.

There are nearly 4.7 million registered nurses nationally (AACN, 2024). Indeed, nurses have always been the largest contingent in the healthcare workforce. Nurses understand the relevance of patient care. They also grasp the financial aspects of providing that care, especially in today's cost-competitive environment. Nurses even move policy. And yet, they are rarely represented on boards.

For this reason, the American Academy of Nursing, the AARP, the American Association of Colleges of Nursing, Sigma Theta Tau International, and many other national organizations formed the Nurses on Boards Coalition (NOBC) in 2014. The mission of this coalition is to increase the presence of nurses on corporate and nonprofit health-related boards of directors throughout the country, including:

- Hospital not-for-profit boards
- Hospital system/network boards

- Hospital foundation boards
- Hospital for-profit boards
- State nurses association boards
- Specialty nursing boards
- EMS/rescue squad boards
- Charitable organization boards
- State peer assistance boards

NOTE

Because the healthcare delivery system and reimbursement models are changing, now is the perfect time for nurses to seek appointment on boards and committees.

NOBC supports placing nurses on boards that impact the health of communities. NOBC collects and shares board openings from both nonprofit and for-profit organizations, including the United Way, municipal and county boards, and pharmaceutical and technology companies. NOBC reports that just under 12,000 nurses have secured board seats as of June 2025. Besides supporting the placement process for a nurse candidate to a board, NOBC offers board preparation and education for nurses interested in or currently serving on a board. Information about these resources is available on the NOBC website (nursesonboardscoalition.org; NOBC, 2025). Specialty organizations are discussed in more detail later in this chapter.

"One person can make a difference, and everyone should try."

–John F. Kennedy

NOTE

Having nurses in key leadership roles—such as on boards and as health commissioners—also boosts their capacity to influence healthcare and health policies. Nurses are in the best position to do this because nursing essentially combines the skills of 20 professionals into one.

Real-World Example: Working With a Governing Board

As a nurse leader, partnering with your hospital board is vital. During my tenure as CNO, I had the good fortune to have a remarkable board. Each member was interested, engaged, committed, and curious. When it came time to discuss new technologies or processes, they wanted to understand how it would impact patients and staff.

A few times a year, we invited frontline nurses to the board meeting to showcase the great work they were doing. I really do not know who enjoyed it more—the nurses or the board members. These board members also sat on a variety of committees that provided grants for special projects. Having a relationship with staff and understanding some of the complexities of care gained from the nurses' presentations served our staff, patients, and organization well.

Some of the processes we demonstrated included a mock delivery with our Victoria mannequin, the demonstration of bedside PICC line insertions with a Sherlock device, the development of patient-friendly medication cards, a device to remind staff to turn patients, dissection of a sheep heart, and the use of a MotoMed2 to ambulate patients on ventilators. Many of these processes went on to win quality and safety awards as well.

In closing, the voice of nursing is valued and respected. Consider going to the NOBC website and see if something piques your interest!

What Is a Specialty Organization?

A *specialty organization* is an organization whose mission pertains to drawing attention to or advancing the causes of a specific professional specialty—for example, nursing. There are several specialty organizations geared toward the nursing profession. Here are a few examples of specialty organizations that relate to nursing specifically or to healthcare in general:

- Emergency Nurses Association
- American Nurses Association
- American Nurses Credentialing Center
- International Nurses Society on Addictions
- American Heart Association
- American Red Cross

Specialty Organization Governing Boards

Like all governing boards, the primary responsibility of the governing board of a specialty organization is to oversee the organization's finances. The governing body for a specialty organization typically consists of a board of directors, the CEO, and nonvoting members, such as the journal editor or the president of the organization's certification board.

As with hospitals and healthcare systems, most specialty organization governing boards have an executive committee. This committee might consist of the following:

- President
- President-elect
- Treasurer
- Secretary

NOTE

Again, titles as well as term limits vary from organization to organization and are dictated by the board's bylaws.

Similar to governing boards for hospitals and healthcare systems, specialty organization boards have committees—for example, for recruitment, fundraising, and educational programming. Ad hoc task forces might also be formed to investigate and report on special issues or circumstances. When their job is complete, these task forces are then dissolved.

The primary responsibilities of a specialty organization's board include:

- Hiring either a full-time executive director or contracting with a management company to manage the organization
- Ensuring fiscal accountability
- Recommending the development of organizational policies and procedures
- Giving final approval on organizational policies and procedures
- Strategic planning
- Fundraising
- Recruiting new members

Just as they can be valuable contributors to the board of a hospital or healthcare system, nurses can play an important role on specialty nursing organization and other healthcare-oriented boards. Nurses do not live in a vacuum; they are part of a community. As such, they know what is going on in healthcare on the local, state, and national level.

I have had the opportunity to serve on a number of boards in my career. I served the Emergency Nurses Association at the local, state, and national level in roles from Director through National President. This was a rewarding and exciting opportunity to serve our members and represent their voices. Currently, I serve on the Board of Nightingales Association of Pennsylvania. This organization provides educational scholarship grants and awards to recognize expertise, professionalism, and dedication to our profession.

Other Types of Committees

In addition to serving on boards, nurses should consider seeking appointment to special committees—for example, a committee of the president of the United States. You might think this would be impossible, but nurses actually have served in such positions!

Specialty Organization Budgets

While we're on the subject of specialty organizations, let's take a moment to discuss their budgets.

You've read about budgeting in detail throughout this book, so I won't repeat basic budgeting information here. Instead, this section discusses budgeting considerations that pertain specifically to specialty organizations.

A specialty nursing organization's financial performance is defined by:

- Total assets
- Total liabilities
- Investments

A specialty nursing organization's revenue may derive from any or all of the following:

- **Membership dues:** Some specialty organizations collect dues from members. This is often an important source of revenue for the organization.

- **Educational offerings:** These are programs offered by the organization. For example, before the International Nurses Society on Addictions annual conference, the organization conducts an Addictions 101 course, for which it charges a fee.
- **Certifications:** Some organizations offer specialty certifications for which individuals must pay. Other revenue might come from prep courses that people take to prepare for certification exams.
- **Journal:** Some organizations publish a journal—for example, on a quarterly, monthly, or bi-annual basis. This can generate revenue or serve as a marketing tool to attract new members. Organizations typically partner with a publisher of some sort to produce the journal. Membership dues usually cover the organization's costs to produce the journal; revenue is typically split between the organization and the publisher.
- **Products/services:** Many organizations sell mugs, T-shirts, and other items that feature the organization's logo.
- **Annual conference:** Conferences can be a major revenue source or a break-even/member value strategy, depending on the organization's model.
- **Other income:** Other income might include donations or grant funding.

A specialty nursing organization's expenses may include any or all of the following:

- **Administrative costs:** These typically pertain to hiring and employing staff (like an executive director) or contracting with a management company (which usually charges a negotiated monthly fee).
- **Board expenses:** These include expenses associated with face-to-face board meetings, travel and hotel accommodations for such meetings, meal expenses, and money spent to send a board member to a conference or program on behalf of the organization.

- **Educational offerings:** These are the costs associated with putting on educational programs.
- **Journal:** These are the costs associated with publishing the journal, including paying the journal's editor. These are usually contracted rates.
- **Marketing products/services:** These are the costs for marketing activities—for example, printing marketing materials or purchasing member lists to determine to whom products and services should be marketed.
- **Annual conference:** These include costs for the conference space; meals; use of equipment such as sound equipment, LCD projectors, and laptops; and so on.
- **Other expenses:** These might include fees for carrying insurance for the board of directors, travel expenses for the executive director, consultant fees, and so on.

Figure 10.1 shows a sample budget for a specialty organization. Review it to see if you can gauge its financial health and performance.

You can see here that revenue exceeded expenses, which is the goal of any well-functioning organization.

Summary

This chapter covered:

- Governing boards
- The responsibilities of a governing board
- Conflicts of interest
- Common mistakes with governing boards

- The role of nurses on governing boards
- Specialty organizations
- Specialty organization governing boards
- Specialty organization budgets

Special thanks to my colleague Nancy Mannion, DNP, RN, CEN, FAEN, FAAN, President of NMB Global Leadership. As Past President of NOBC, her input was invaluable!

References

American Association of Colleges of Nursing. (2024, April). *Nursing workforce fact sheet.* https://www.aacnnursing.org/news-data/fact-sheets/nursing-workforce-fact-sheet

American Hospital Association. (2026). *Getting nurses on board(s).* AHA Trustee Services. https://trustees.aha.org/getting-nurses-boards#:~:text=The%20AHA%202022%20National%20Health,to%20serve%20in%20board%20roles

Nurses on Boards Coalition. (2025). *Overview.* https://acrobat.adobe.com/link/track?uri=urn:aaid:scds:US:80bd798f-7027-353f-9dad-636ba813155c

	2024 ACTUAL	2024 Budget	2025 ACTUAL	2025 Budget	2026 Budget
Income					
Journal Royalty	15,000.00	15,000.00	15,000.00	15,000.00	15,000.00
Conference Income	34,160.12	25,417.00	30,340.00	37,700.00	33,825.00
Investment Income	152.69	25.00	3.05	5.00	5.00
Marketing					
Ad Type 1	1,200.00	500.00	3,600.00	1,200.00	3,600.00
Ad Type 2	3,075.00	3,500.00	3,170.00	3,000.00	2,375.00
Total Marketing	4,275.00	4,000.00	6,770.00	4,200.00	5,975.00
Membership Dues					
Member Type 1	8,265.00	5,130.00	10,024.00	6,650.00	9,400.00
Member Type 2	700.00	1,200.00	120.00	0.00	120.00
Member Type 3	48,689.50	45,825.00	45,614.00	48,175.00	47,000.00
Member Type 4	1,320.00	1,760.00	801.00	660.00	1,100.00
Member Type 5	0.00	0.00	1,336.00	600.00	625.00
Total Membership Dues	58,974.50	53,915.00	57,895.00	56,085.00	58,245.00
Sales	485.00	400.00	165.00	450.00	150.00
Total Income	113,047.31	98,757.00	110,173.05	113,440.00	113,200.00
Expense					
Bank Fees	27.70	0.00	0.00	50.00	50.00
Board of Directors					
Awards	590.77	250.00	559.90	750.00	600.00
Gifts	281.10	0.00	199.71	350.00	250.00
Meetings	0.00	1,300.00	640.95	1,300.00	1,500.00
Miscellaneous	575.29	200.00	0.00	0.00	0.00
Staff Travel	1,457.58	950.00	877.10	750.00	1,000.00
Total Board of Directors	2,904.74	2,700.00	2,277.66	3,150.00	3,350.00

	2024 ACTUAL	2024 Budget	2025 ACTUAL	2025 Budget	2026 Budget
Conference Expenses	33,403.58	37,954.00	33,616.56	31,950.00	33,600.00
Credit Card Transactions					
Monthly/Yearly Fees	360.00	0.00	360.00	360.00	360.00
Transaction Fees	1,985.90	1,000.00	2,188.72	2,500.00	2,500.00
Total Credit Card Transactions	2,345.90	1,000.00	2,548.72	2,860.00	2,860.00
Journal Publication	4,241.52	3,000.00	0.00	3,500.00	3,500.00
Legal/Professional Fees					
Accountant	400.00	715.00	0.00	650.00	650.00
Corporate Filings	80.00	0.00	120.00	80.00	150.00
Insurance	2,455.00	1,771.00	3,026.00	2,500.00	3,050.00
Miscellaneous	0.00	0.00	0.00	0.00	100.00
Total Legal/Professional Fees	2,935.00	2,486.00	3,146.00	3,230.00	3,950.00
Management Fee	41,445.00	40,800.00	43,656.00	43,656.00	43,656.00
Office Expenses					
Conference Calls	91.20	150.00	0.00	0.00	0.00
Copies/Printing	342.74	1,150.00	291.32	450.00	300.00
Fax	13.80	0.00	4.40	15.00	10.00
Graphic Design	1,169.50	0.00	985.00	250.00	250.00
Promotional Emails	346.86	498.00	525.00	350.00	550.00
Postage	1,063.18	600.00	211.33	600.00	250.00
Scans	23.40	0.00	69.20	50.00	75.00
Supplies	0.00	250.00	157.00	0.00	0.00
Telephone	305.86	725.00	80.07	325.00	100.00
Web Hosting	3,160.56	1,450.00	559.70	850.00	600.00
Total Office Expenses	6,517.10	4,823.00	2,883.02	2,890.00	2,135.00
Sales Expense	40.28	150.00	0.00	850.00	100.00
Total Expense	93,860.82	92,913.00	88,127.96	92,136.00	93,201.00
Net Income	**19,186.49**	**5,844.00**	**22,045.09**	**21,304.00**	**19,999.00**

FIGURE 10.1
A sample specialty nursing organization budget.

Improving Quality and Safety to Increase Reimbursement

Quality is a key concern for all healthcare providers and organizations. Absolutely no one wants adverse patient outcomes! Examples of adverse patient outcomes include:

- Wrong-site surgeries
- Wrong medication
- Prescribing errors
- Transcribing errors
- Poor communication (both written and verbal)
- Healthcare-associated infections (HAIs)

> *"Quality is everyone's responsibility."*
>
> *–W. Edwards Deming*

Adverse outcomes aren't just bad for patients; they're also bad for healthcare organizations. This is because adverse outcomes often bring with them increased costs and lower reimbursements. *Iatrogenic* events are illnesses or other medical problems caused by the healthcare system itself, which often result in prolonged and costly hospital stays. Some payers deny payment for specific preventable complications (e.g., certain hospital-acquired conditions) or reduce payment via value-based programs, but overall payment impact is program- and payer-specific (e.g., penalties/withholds, denied incremental payment for certain conditions, risk contracts, etc.).

Iatrogenic Events

The *Journal of Patient Safety* estimated that between 210,000 and 440,000 patients die each year from iatrogenic effects after presenting themselves in a healthcare setting (James, 2013). More recently, studies have found between 10% and 25% of all patients treated in a healthcare setting will experience an adverse event caused by medical management (Bates et al., 2023; Skelly et al., 2025). The United States has a higher incidence of iatrogenic events than other developed nations (Skelly et al., 2025).

Generally speaking, the lower the quality of care provided, the higher the potential risk to the healthcare organization, which often results in higher costs. For example, consider the costs involved with a patient who develops a stage IV pressure ulcer while in the hospital. Improving quality, then, is imperative for any healthcare organization. That's what this chapter is about.

NOTE

One major force behind quality-improvement initiatives in hospitals is the Institute of Medicine (IOM, now called the National Academy of Medicine). The IOM's reports To Err Is Human *(1999) and* Crossing the Quality Chasm *(2001), which laid out in graphic numbers the shocking scale of iatrogenic events, have been key drivers of quality improvement in hospitals.*

Quality and Safety Education for Nurses

In 2005, in response to adverse patient outcomes and public perceptions of the quality of healthcare in the US, the University of North Carolina at Chapel Hill launched a multiphase ongoing project called Quality and Safety Education for Nurses (QSEN). As its name suggests, this project focuses on quality and safety—and nursing's contributions to both—in a healthcare setting. The goal of QSEN is to improve the quality and safety of healthcare delivered to patients.

QSEN has outlined core competencies consisting of knowledge, skills, and attitudes (KSAs) that all prelicensure nursing students should master. (QSEN competencies have also been developed for graduate nursing students.) These are based on competencies identified by the IOM (2003). The six core competencies, or KSAs, are as follows (QSEN Institute, 2022):

- **Patient-centered care:** This KSA recognizes that the patient is a full partner in the provision of compassionate and coordinated care. This competency addresses the patient's preferences, values, and needs.
- **Teamwork and collaboration:** This KSA recognizes that care is delivered through interprofessional teams. Teamwork and collaboration must involve open communication, mutual respect, and shared decision-making, with the ultimate goal of improved patient care and quality outcomes.
- **Evidence-based practice:** This KSA recognizes that nurses must integrate the best current evidence with clinical expertise and incorporate patient/family preferences and values in the delivery of optimal patient care.
- **Quality improvement:** This KSA recognizes that the outcomes of care processes are monitored and evaluated with data so that improvement methods are designed, tested, and implemented to continuously improve the quality and safety of patient care delivered in healthcare systems.

- **Safety:** This KSA recognizes that the risk of harm is minimized to patients and providers through both the effectiveness of the system and the performance of individual providers.
- **Informatics:** This KSA recognizes that informatics should be used to communicate, improve knowledge, and mitigate error. In addition, it supports clinical, administrative, educational, and research-oriented decision-making. Key metrics must be defined by the organization. Finally, data must be mined, which is made possible by good informatics systems.

NOTE

Education is a significant component of QSEN.

Mastering QSEN core competencies and implementing them throughout a healthcare system typically leads to improved reimbursement and thus sounder financial health. This becomes critical when one considers the following points put forth by the Centers for Medicare & Medicaid Services (CMS, 2024):

- The dollar amount spent on healthcare in the US exceeds that of any other nation in the world at $4.9 trillion, or $14,570 per person as of 2023 (CMS, 2024). Because the US has an entrepreneurial healthcare system, administrative costs are much higher here than in other countries.
- Healthcare costs are a significant share of the gross domestic product at 17.6% (CMS, 2024).
- Hospital care (both inpatient and outpatient) is the most significant service with higher costs.

QSEN Competencies and Budgeting

How do the QSEN competencies relate to finances and budgeting from the nurse manager's point of view? The answer is simple. Improved quality is tied to improved outcomes, which lead to more satisfied patients and lower costs. Because nurse managers are held accountable for performance and budgetary measures and metrics, they must be familiar with these competencies.

Incentivizing Quality

Financial incentives that reward good quality and penalize poor quality is one strategy to improve quality and decrease costs. An example is value-based incentives. These might include the following:

- **Transparency:** This enables consumers to select healthcare facilities and systems based on quality and performance as well as cost.
- **Bundled payments:** With this approach, instead of each provider submitting a bill, there is one set rate for the services provided—in other words, a bundled bill.
- **Hospital readmission programs:** These track readmissions that occur within 30 days of a patient being discharged. They then alert the organization to assess whether the patient was discharged too soon, appropriate care was rendered, and hospital discharge instructions were accurate.
- **Hospital inpatient value-based purchasing (VBP) programs:** These relate to the value of care provided. Providing high-quality care improves patient outcomes. For example, a post-operative cardiac patient should not sustain a sternal wound infection.
- **Hospital-acquired conditions programs:** These relate to events that happen in the hospital that should not have occurred—for example, a patient getting a urinary tract infection or sustaining a fall with a resultant injury.

Bundled Payments

Medicare uses the diagnosis-related group system to bill for inpatient acute care hospitalization. This is a form of bundled payment. With this system, a case rate is used rather than per diem charges. Under the Patient Protection and Affordable Care Act, a bundle may include only one payment per event or one payment per patient per year to an accountable care organization (ACO). This results in a form of capitated payment.

Notice that the preceding list includes hospital VBP programs. These entail the following:

- Payment for care beyond just the volume of care delivered
- Payment for care that rewards better value, patient outcomes, and innovation
- Evaluation and scoring of performance, which is added into the payment system

Nursing-Sensitive Value-Based Purchasing

Nursing-sensitive VBP seeks to optimize staffing and the healthcare practice environment through outcome incentives and transparency of structure, process, and patient outcome measures. This initiative:

- Establishes core measures
- Improves Hospital Consumer Assessment of Healthcare Providers and Systems (HCAHPS) overall scores
- Improves hospital VBP scores
- Affects Medicare reimbursement to the hospital
- Recognizes the criticality of nursing to improved quality of patient care

Hospital VBP programs typically receive payment based on the metrics shown in Figure 11.1.

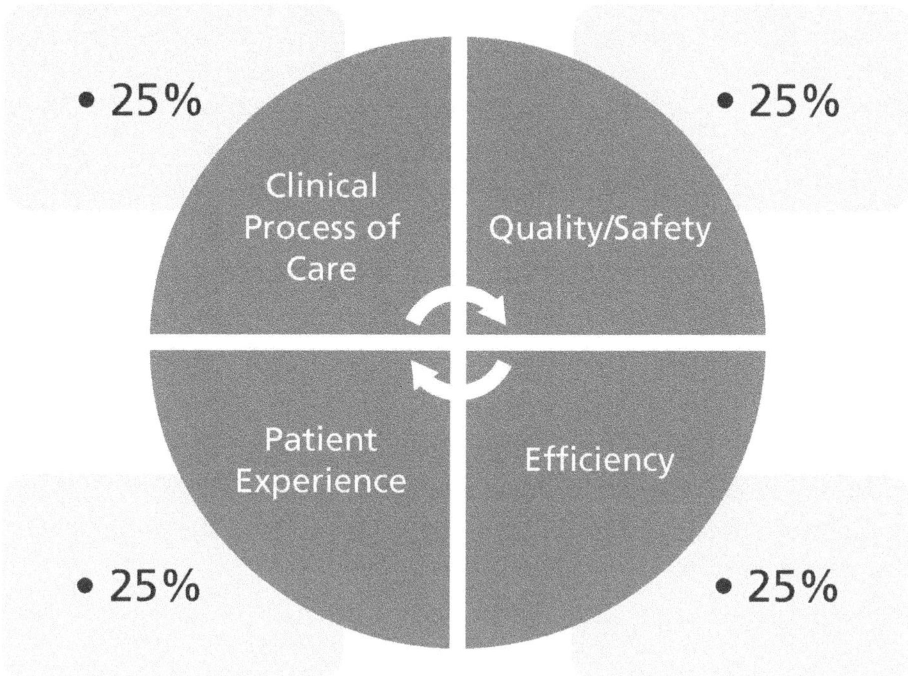

FIGURE 11.1
Reimbursement model under a hospital-based purchasing program (© Al Rundio, 2020).

NOTE

Medicare uses this same basic model for its VBP reimbursements.

Essentially, the total performance score dictates reimbursement. In the hospital VBP program, CMS withholds a portion of the reimbursement (such as 2%) and redistributes it based on performance (see Figure 11.2).

FIGURE 11.2
Total performance score = reimbursement.

The following sections discuss the clinical process of care and the patient experience in more detail.

The Clinical Process of Care

The clinical process of care typically follows an algorithmic approach. For example, suppose a 55-year-old man enters the hospital emergency department (ED) with chest pain. To achieve the 25% reimbursement mark, certain care processes must be implemented:

- The patient's vital signs must be taken.
- An intravenous line will be inserted.
- An EKG will be done.
- Lab work, such as a cardiac enzyme test, troponin test, international normalized ratio test, chemistry profile, complete blood count, and so on, will be done.
- The patient will receive a portable chest X-ray.
- The patient will be administered morphine, oxygen, nitroglycerin, and aspirin therapy, if appropriate. (Remember: This reflects the steps in treatment but not the order in which you must perform them.)

- If the EKG is positive for myocardial infarction, the patient will be administered fibrinolytic therapy within 30 minutes of arrival to the ED or receive a percutaneous cardiac intervention—that is, angioplasty and stent placement—within 90 minutes of arrival to the ED.

If healthcare providers omit any step in this process, the healthcare facility will receive less reimbursement because the process of care was not followed explicitly.

The Patient Experience

The patient experience is evaluated based on a number of factors, including the following:

- HCAHPS scores
- Nurse communication
- Physician communication
- Hospital staff responsiveness
- Medication management
- Quality of pain management
- Hospital cleanliness
- Discharge information
- Overall hospital rating
- Whether quality metrics are met
- Whether zero events requirements are met
- Efficiency
- Whether the patient was transferred from the ED to an appropriate level of care
- Whether the OR schedule of cases started on time

A point is assigned to each measure or dimension. Rates are then compared for the performance period against the baseline period.

NOTE

HCAHPS scores reveal the quality of hospital care provided. Public reporting enhances accountability in healthcare.

Other Organizations Pushing for Improved Quality of Care

In addition to insurers and healthcare organizations, entities such as the following are also driving initiatives to improve care:

- **The Leapfrog Group:** This organization is arguably the premiere nonprofit watchdog group that focuses on transparency in healthcare, which it believes will lead to more informed consumers and better outcomes across the board.
- ***U.S. News & World Report:*** This organization ranks hospitals both nationally and regionally on an annual basis for the quality of care and services provided. It also ranks individual specialties such as neuro, ortho, cardiac, and so on.
- **Hospital Safety Score:** This grades hospitals on how safe they keep their patients from errors, injuries, accidents, and infections.
- ***Consumer Reports:*** This organization publishes hospital ratings to help consumers compare hospitals based on patient safety scores, the patient experience, patient outcomes, and certain hospital practices.
- **National Quality Forum:** This nonprofit membership organization promotes patient protections and healthcare quality through measurement and public reporting. It also provides research recommendations designed to improve the quality of healthcare.

A few regulating and accrediting agencies have even mandated the incentivization of quality. These include:

- **Det Norske Veritas (DNV):** This certification body works with healthcare organizations around the world to minimize risk and maximize opportunities for excellence through safety and quality. For more information about DNV, see https://www.dnv.com/.
- **The Joint Commission:** This organization accredits and certifies healthcare facilities and programs for quality. The goal of the JCAH is to improve quality care for patients. For more information about the JCAH, see https://www.jointcommission.org/about-us/.
- **State departments of health:** State departments of health conduct health facility evaluations. How these are conducted varies from each state. For example, one state might survey every healthcare facility once annually. Another might accept a voluntary certification or accreditation and only perform a site visit if there is a specific patient complaint. Surveys with state departments of health are involuntary, as these entities grant licensure to healthcare facilities so that they can operate in a particular state. For more information, visit any of the various state department of health websites.

The Role of Nursing in Improving Quality

The following list identifies nursing areas and concepts that have been proven to work to improve the safety and quality of patient care:

- Safe staffing
- An appropriate and sufficient skill mix in staff
- Teamwork

- Trust
- Accountability
- Transparency
- Exceptional nursing leadership

You might wonder how all this relates to QSEN competencies. The following list explains how:

- Cost savings can be achieved when adverse events are decreased.
- Cost savings can be achieved when hospital readmissions are prevented.
- Nursing is critical to the reductions of adverse patient events and hospital readmissions.
- Nurses spend the most time with patients; thus, improving the quality of nursing care is crucial.

The following factors related to the structure of nursing care can affect outcomes:

- Supply of nursing staff
- Skill level of nursing staff
- Education level of nursing staff
- Certification of nursing staff

Staffing and Quality

The goal in the healthcare delivery system is to improve quality while at the same time decreasing costs. For many nurse managers, this means increasing staffing. But the reality is, more staff doesn't necessarily mean the best staff mix for the setting. At the same time, if there is too little staff, patient care might not be up to par. Research evidence has demonstrated that the right mix of staff in nursing is critical. For example, organizations with a higher RN-to-patient ratio tend to have better outcomes because RNs are more accountable and can do more than other levels of staff. These same institutions have lower costs.

Nursing care should seek to provide optimal care while also avoiding HAIs. Processes to help avoid these include:

- **Handwashing:** Good handwashing can help nurses avoid HAIs. Removing bacteria from their hands before they touch a patient prevents cross-contamination.
- **Proper sterilization of instruments:** This prevents infections secondary to procedures.
- **Proper refrigeration of food:** This prevents foodborne illnesses.
- **Judicious use of antibiotics:** This helps prevent resistance patterns of bacteria and other organisms.

Nursing care has an impact on the following factors, which are evaluated in an outcome-incentivized scheme:

- Prevention of infections, including surgical site infections, ventilator-associated pneumonia, and catheter-associated urinary tract infections
- Prevention of stage III and stage IV decubitus ulcers
- Prevention of falls, including falls with injury
- Length of stay in the ICU
- Readmissions

Nursing care is critical to financial reimbursement and thus to the entire budgeting system of any healthcare organization or system. Reimbursement is based on bundled billing, on the achievement of clinical indicators, and on patient experience. Nursing and nursing-sensitive indicators are critical to all these. Simply put, nursing is crucial to the provision of excellent patient care, making quality nursing care essential for hospital survival.

NOTE

The quest for quality includes creating a just culture, in which nurses are not afraid to report iatrogenic events and other negative outcomes or practices.

The Quintuple Aim

We cannot consider quality in healthcare without considering the contributions of the Quintuple Aim framework. Pioneered by Don Berwick and the Institute for Healthcare Improvement (IHI), this simple framework, originally the Triple Aim, transformed how healthcare organizations started to organize and explore their improvement efforts (Quintuple Aim Solutions, 2024). The original focus was on improving the patient experience of healthcare, improving the health of populations, and reducing per capita costs. However, later contributions recognized that clinician health and well-being impacted overall patient safety and quality, and the framework was expanded to include improving the work life of healthcare providers (the Quadruple Aim). It is a well-known fact that happy staff = happy patients. Those of us working in healthcare see things that are morally, ethically, and emotionally stressful every day as we help our patients navigate difficult healthcare challenges. Ensuring that our healthcare system recognizes and responds to these stressors is essential for the future well-being of our professions. The most recent addition to the framework is advancing health equity, thus making five "aims" in total (Gould, 2022; Nundy et al., 2022) for healthcare organizations to design and assess solutions to improve healthcare. This new imperative addresses unique healthcare challenges of populations that are often socially marginalized—minorities, the elderly, patients in chronic care, and those who live in poverty. In an article from Quintuple Aim Solutions (2024), the Quintuple Aim is depicted as a pyramid similar to Maslow's hierarchy of needs (see Figure 11.3).

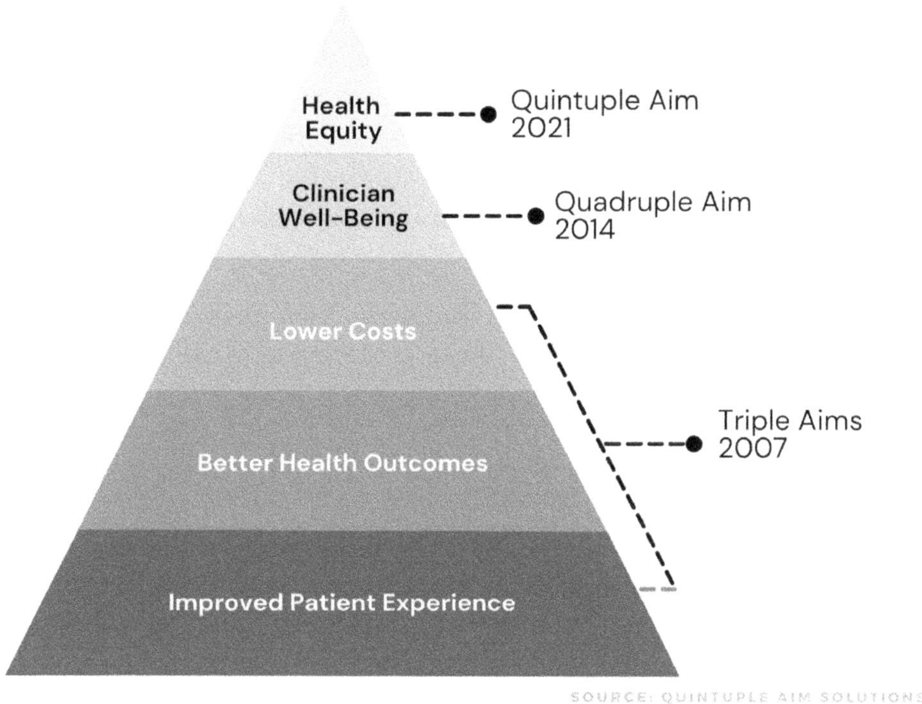

FIGURE 11.3
The five aims of the Quintuple Aim framework.
(Nundy et al., 2022. For more about the IHI Quintuple Aim, visit ihi.org.)

Our world of healthcare is changing every minute of every day. I am sure that the Quintuple Aim will continue to evolve as well. At the current time, it represents a fundamental shift in our healthcare to support a more inclusive, just, and caring system. Each healthcare system will have unique challenges depending on the populations they serve. This additional initiative shifts the paradigm and redefines the meaning of quality. Organizations must listen to those close to the care for innovative and creative solutions. As nurse managers and leaders, each of you is uniquely positioned to hear the voices of those closest to the care and bring those ideas forward, utilizing effective communication as well as your finely tuned budgeting skills!

Quality and Population Health

In my experience, the US has historically focused primarily on quality in hospitals. Recently, however, there's been increased attention on quality as it pertains to population health. *Population health* refers to the health of a group of individuals in a community. Ascertaining population health involves applying key metrics about the community in question.

Improving population health is vitally important to achieving excellent quality outcomes for patients. It makes sense, then, that some hospitals and healthcare systems in the US have begun attempting to influence population health.

Population Health in Action

Recently, a quality-improvement team from an acute care hospital visited elder homes in the community it served. Team members noticed that the bathtubs in many of these homes did not have shower bars, which increased residents' risk of falling. So, the hospital paid to install shower bars in all bathrooms in these homes that did not already have them.

Assessing Home Care Quality

Home care is a critical component of any ACO. Insurance companies will generally pay for home care services because these services are typically less costly than—and can even prevent—hospital admissions.

Home care services generally include the following:

- Skilled nursing care
- Nursing aid care
- Nutritional services
- Rehabilitation services
- Social services

In 2018, CMS released a new rating and search system for the evaluation of home care and other healthcare services called Care Compare (https://www.medicare.gov/care-compare/#search). Ratings are based on specific criteria that focus on the quality of patient care and the patient survey for providers of home care services. Making these ratings public empowers consumers to compare home care providers and select the one that best serves their needs.

NOTE

The highest rating that a home care agency can achieve is a 5-star rating.

CMS uses two methods to assess home care agencies. One method evaluates statistical reports (including OASIS data) from home care agencies about staff treatment of patients and patient improvement. There are seven measures in the Quality of Patient Care Star Rating:

1. Timely initiation of care (process measure)
2. Improvement in ambulation (outcome measure)
3. Improvement in bed transferring (outcome measure)
4. Improvement in bathing (outcome measure)
5. Improvement in shortness of breath (outcome measure)

6. Improvement in management of oral medications (outcome measure)
7. Home health within stay potentially preventable hospitalization (PPH) (outcome measure)

(CMS, 2026)

The other method relies on data from patient surveys about their experiences with home care services. The Patient Survey Star Rating is based on the patient's answers on a 25-item survey evaluating areas such as:

- Whether the patient received care in a timely manner
- Whether the patient was provided with information and education about their medications
- Whether the care provider(s) discussed ways to adapt the patient's home for greater safety
- Whether the care provider(s) treated the patient with kindness, made them feel cared for as a person, and handled them as gently and respectfully as possible
- Whether the care provider(s) was knowledgeable of the patient's specific care needs and medical history
- Whether the care provider(s) communicated well with the patient, listened, and answered questions and made sure the patient understood what was communicated
- Whether the care provider(s) communicated well with family or friends and provided them with necessary instructions or explanations

(Consumer Assessment of Healthcare Providers and Systems, 2026)

The five top-rated states/districts for long-term care as of 2024 were (Shuman & Shevik, 2025):

- Minnesota
- Washington
- Washington, DC
- Massachusetts
- Colorado

NOTE

As you can clearly see from this discussion, CMS and the federal government are most concerned with the quality of care that patients receive, the patient experience, and patients' evaluation of such.

High-Reliability Organizations

Although quality improvement efforts have been effective, completely eradicating human error is impossible. The reality is that human beings make mistakes. Moreover, medicine—including nursing—is not an exact science. In an effort to prevent human error, many hospitals are now attempting to become what they call *high-reliability organizations.*

The goal of high-reliability organizations is to consistently provide high levels of safety and quality across all healthcare services and settings. They achieve this by implementing mindful processes to eliminate variability in outcomes and therefore experience an absolute minimum number of errors. There are five principles of a high-reliability organization:

1. **Preoccupation with Failure:** pay close attention to "near misses," be alert for workarounds, everyone should always be looking for opportunities to improve

2. **Reluctance to Simplify:** challenge the status quo, constantly examine data and performance measures
3. **Sensitivity to Operations:** practice situational awareness, create opportunities to engage all members of the organization, intentional rounding
4. **Commitment to Resilience:** learn to manage the unexpected
5. **Deference to Expertise:** listen to the experts, engage the front line, value expertise over authority

(Jacobson, 2025)

NOTE

Some high-reliability organizations strive for zero errors. This target might be unrealistic, however, because the human factor is always present.

To achieve high-reliability organization status, organizations must consider the following:

- Creating a culture of safety and quality that involves continuous learning
- Creating a culture of caring that encourages transparency so that problems can quickly be identified and action immediately taken to prevent future incidents
- Instituting action-oriented reviews that comprehensively evaluate safety performance data
- Instituting peer reviews so that everyone's performance is continuously evaluated
- Stamping out disruptive behaviors and substandard performance

- Raising the performance bar so that everyone in the organization continually tries to improve themselves as well as others
- Being collaborative
- Being transparent in reporting performance to regulators and other agencies

(Murray et al., 2024)

NOTE

QSEN provides the KSAs needed to foster high reliability and minimize errors.

Historically, healthcare organizations have tended to take a reactive approach to quality—that is, they try to improve quality only after a major negative event has occurred. In contrast, high-reliability organizations are proactive. They identify conditions or issues that might affect quality *before* a negative event happens. This proactive approach inevitably results in improved reimbursement. It also creates satisfied patients and drives positive word of mouth. All this means healthier finances and the sustained growth of a healthcare organization.

"Quality is more important than quantity. One home run is better than two doubles."

–Steve Jobs

Summary

This chapter covered:

- Quality and Safety Education for Nurses
- Incentivizing quality
- The role of nursing in improving quality

- Quality and population health
- Assessing home care quality
- High-reliability organizations

References

Bates, D. W., Levine, D. M., Salmasian, H., Syrowatka, A., Shahain, D. M., Lipsitz, S., Zebrowski, J. P., Myers, L. C., Logan, M. S., Roy, C. G., Iannaccone, C., Frits, M. L., Volk, L. A., Dulgarian, S., Amato, M. G., Edress, H. H., Sato, L., Folcarelli, P., Einbinder, J. S., Reynolds, M. E., & Mort, E. (2023). The safety of inpatient health care. *New England Journal of Medicine, 388*(2), 142–153. https://doi.org/10.1056/nejmsa2206117

Centers for Medicare & Medicaid Services. (2024, June 24). *NHE fact sheet.* https://www.cms.gov/data-research/statistics-trends-and-reports/national-health-expenditure-data/nhe-fact-sheet

Centers for Medicare & Medicaid Services. (2026, Feb. 3). *Home health star ratings.* https://www.cms.gov/medicare/quality/home-health/home-health-star-ratings

Consumer Assessment of Healthcare Providers and Systems. (2026). *Home health care CAHPS survey.* https://homehealthcahps.org/Portals/0/SurveyMaterials/HHCAHPS_Questionnaire_English.pdf

Gould, K. A. (2022). Equity: Introducing the Quintuple Aim. *Dimensions of Critical Care Nursing, 41*(3), 119–120. https://doi.org/10.1097/dcc.0000000000000527

Institute of Medicine. (1999). *To err is human: Building a safer health system.* National Academies Press.

Institute of Medicine. (2001). *Crossing the quality chasm: A new health system for the 21st century.* National Academies Press.

Institute of Medicine. (2003). *Health professions education: A bridge to quality.* National Academies Press.

Jacobson, G. (2025, July 16). 5 principles of high-reliability organizations, explained [Blog]. *KaiNexus.* https://blog.kainexus.com/improvement-disciplines/hro/5-principles

James, J. T. (2013). A new, evidence-based estimate of patient harms associated with hospital care. *Journal of Patient Safety*, *9*(3), 122–128. https://doi.org/10.1097/pts.0b013e3182948a69

Murray, J. S., Baghdadi, A., Dannenberg, W., Crews, P., & Walsh, N. D. (2024). The role of high reliability organization foundational practices in building a culture of safety. *Federal Practitioner, 41*(7), 214–221. https://doi.org/10.12788/fp.0486

Nundy, S., Cooper, L. A., & Mate, K. S. (2022). The Quintuple Aim for health care improvement: A new imperative to advance health equity. *JAMA, 327*(6), 521–522. https://doi.org/10.1001/jama.2021.25181

QSEN Institute. (2022). *QSEN Institute competencies.* https://www.qsen.org/competencies-pre-licensure-ksas

Quintuple Aim Solutions. (2024, July 2). *The Quintuple Aims.* https://www.quintupleaim.com/blog/the-quintuple-aims

Shuman, T., & Shevik, J. (2025, November 17). *2024 senior healthcare state report cards.* Senior Living. https://www.seniorliving.org/research/best-states-senior-healthcare/

Skelly, C. L., McMahon, K., & Munakomi, S. (2025, Aug. 2). Adverse events. *StatPearls.* https://www.ncbi.nlm.nih.gov/books/NBK558963

CHAPTER 12

Artificial Intelligence Budgeting Considerations

By **Nicholas Chmielewski,** DNP, RN, CEN, CENP, NEA-BC, FAEN

The term *artificial intelligence* (AI) commonly refers to the application of machine learning techniques to large datasets (predictive modeling) and the emergence of computer systems generating content (generative tools). At the time of this publication, AI's use is rapidly expanding in healthcare, both in aiding/supporting clinical practice and in administrative supporting functions (see Table 12.1). This chapter discusses AI policy, budget, and use considerations for the nurse manager.

> *"As more and more artificial intelligence is entering into the world, more and more emotional intelligence must enter into leadership."*
>
> *–Amit Ray*

TABLE 12.1 EXAMPLES OF AI'S EMERGING USE IN HEALTHCARE

Staffing and scheduling	Predictive scheduling: Analyzes historical staffing data and patient volumes to create optimal schedules
	Workload balancing: Identifies overworked units or staff and recommends adjustments
	Absenteeism forecasting: Predicts sick leaves or burnout risk to proactively manage staff shortages
Operations and workflow optimization	Resource allocation: Predicts patient flow and resource needs (beds, equipment, supplies)
	Task automation: Automates routine documentation, reminders, and reporting (e.g., shift change reports)
	Process improvement: Identifies bottlenecks in clinical workflows and suggests improvements
	Statistical analysis: Automates statistical analysis by selecting appropriate statistical tests via a decision tree; some tools can also generate plain-English summaries or interpretations of results and create tables and figures in different documentation formats (e.g., APA, AMA)
Clinical decision support	Triage tools: Helps nurses prioritize patients by severity using AI-driven risk stratification
	Alerts and reminders: Flags abnormal lab results or missed treatments in real time
	Evidence-based recommendations: Pulls from updated clinical guidelines and patient data to support treatment planning
Predictive analytics for patient care	Early warning systems: Predicts patient deterioration (e.g., sepsis, falls) based on real-time vitals and EHR data
	Readmission risk: Identifies patients at high risk for readmission so proactive care can be provided
	Length of stay forecasting: Helps plan discharge and resource utilization

Staff education and performance monitoring	Skill gap analysis: Analyzes performance data to identify training needs Personalized learning: Recommends training modules based on individual competencies Feedback analysis: Analyzes staff or patient feedback for quality improvement insights
Documentation and administrative tasks	Natural language processing: Transcribes and summarizes clinical notes Smart dashboards: Curates key metrics like patient satisfaction, infection rates, or staff turnover for decision-making Automated report generation: Speeds up compliance and audit documentation Performs generative tasks (e.g., drafting reports) Accelerates speed and content in email responses Assists in meeting minute generation (summarizing) Assists in preparing for an upcoming meeting or day's calendar Converts files from one format to another (e.g., converting content from a spreadsheet to a presentation slide, or from a slide presentation to an email or narrative format)
Communication and patient engagement	AI chatbots: Handles FAQs for patients or families, reducing call volumes Translation tools: Performs real-time language translation for multicultural settings Sentiment analysis: Understands emotional tone of patient feedback to identify service issues
Quality and risk management	Error detection: Identifies patterns in medication errors or near misses Policy compliance monitoring: Flags deviations from protocols or safety practices Incident prediction: Predicts likelihood of adverse events (falls, infections, etc.)

Legal and Organizational Policy

Responsible AI use begins with understanding and respecting the legal and organizational boundaries in place at your institution. Before implementing any machine learning techniques or AI tools, it is essential to review your organization's AI use policy to both ensure compliance and protect sensitive data. These policies can range from outright bans to detailed guidelines on appropriate use, often requiring employees to use only organization-approved AI platforms within the organization's digitally secure environment. For instance, using Microsoft Copilot on an enterprise-managed platform for business purposes may be permitted, while accessing a personal version for the same tasks could pose serious risks to data integrity and security. Unauthorized use of AI platforms can lead to breaches involving protected health information (PHI), employee records, or other sensitive data, potentially violating HIPAA and other regulatory standards. Additionally, recording meetings or deploying AI technologies in two-party consent states without explicit permission from each participant is legally problematic. Given the rapid evolution of AI, it's critical to seek clarification on your organization's policies on use of specific software, data boundary controls, and recording/transcription, or any other ambiguous areas before proceeding.

IT Security Review and Approval

Your organization will likely have an IT security clearance process that must be navigated for new products to be deemed appropriate for use by the organization. Some elements of the core IT security requirements for the AI use approval process include:

- **Data governance and classification**
    - Identify and classify data types (e.g., PII, PHI, financial data) that the specific AI system may access.
    - Ensure AI tools are configured to handle only approved data categories.

- **Access controls and authentication**
  - Enforce role-based access to AI platforms.
  - Require multi-factor authentication for users interacting with AI systems.
- **Approved platform usage**
  - Mandate use of enterprise-approved AI platforms only.
  - Prohibit use of personal or consumer-grade AI tools for business operations to prevent data leakage.
- **Encryption and secure transmission**
  - Encrypt data in transit and at rest when processed by AI systems.
  - Use secure protocols for AI integration.
- **Audit trails and monitoring**
  - Maintain detailed logs of AI interactions and data usage.
  - Monitor for anomalies, unauthorized access, or misuse of AI capabilities.
- **Compliance with regulations**
  - Ensure AI use aligns with HIPAA, GDPR, CCPA, and other applicable laws, depending on which applies to your region.
  - Avoid using AI for recording or transcription in jurisdictions requiring two-party consent unless all parties agree.
- **Third-party risk management**
  - Vet AI vendors for security certifications (e.g., SOC 2, ISO 27001, HITRUST).
  - Establish data processing agreements and review vendor privacy policies.

- **Policy awareness and training**
  - Educate employees on organizational AI policies and security protocols.
  - Require periodic training on responsible AI use and data protection.
- **Incident response planning**
  - Include AI-related risks in incident response and disaster recovery plans.
  - Define procedures for handling breaches involving AI systems.

As AI technologies evolve, organizations must continuously update their IT security frameworks to address emerging threats and maintain trust.

Operational Budget

There are a few different ways healthcare organizations budget their AI tools, commonly grouped into one of three categories:

1. **Corporate enterprise:** The organization groups all software-related expenses (licenses, subscriptions, maintenance fees) as one expense grouped under IT. The costs may be centralized under the IT department or cost-allocated to individual units. Example: An enterprise-wide EHR vendor such as Epic or Cerner retains costs at the corporate level, and they are not passed down to the individual cost center.
2. **Corporate enterprise subscription with cost allocation:** In this scenario, the corporation negotiates an enterprise subscription to a service that is charged on a per-use or per-license basis, which is then passed down as a charge to the cost center. See the allocation methods section for further details. Examples:

- A disease detection product charges the organization x dollars per ED visit, billed monthly; this charge is then passed down to the ED cost center.
- A Microsoft Copilot license is a common example used in this scenario because the top-tier version is often structured on a per-license/user per month basis. To adequately manage costs, the nurse manager may want to limit the top-tier version to just their leadership team, which may or may not include charge nurses based on their administrative responsibilities. Individual use patterns in license-based products should be reviewed at least annually to determine if the continued expense is warranted.

3. **Individual authorized subscriptions charged to the cost center:** In this scenario, the cost is either passed through from IT directly to the cost center, or the cost center issues its own PO for purchasing. This would likely be used when the software is either a minor use and/or limited to an individual department. An example of this would be AI statistics calculation software for assessing/writing/summarizing performance outcomes on a quality improvement project.

Allocation Methods

While some organizations are discontinuing the practice of department-level cost allocations, there are a variety of methods that can be used if the organization sustains the practice. These include allocating based on flat even distribution, usage-based, per FTE, per patient, or per bed.

Depending on organizational internal accounting structures and/or the product involved, associated costs at the department level are often charged to one of three places: IT expenses or IT services, non-medical administrative supplies, or licenses and fees.

Lastly, it's important to understand whether the product is being invoiced as a one-time charge or an ongoing subscription. Depending on institutional practices, one-time charges may be treated as capital and spread over several years per finance policy.

Summary

This chapter discussed:

- AI's expanding role as a useful tool for a variety of purposes
- Legal and policy compliance for responsible AI use
- IT security to ensure safe and effective AI deployment
- AI budgeting and allocation models
- Continuous improvement to address new risks and maintain trust

NOTE

Disclosure: During the preparation of this chapter, the author used Microsoft Copilot to (1) synthesize and organize common themes among multiple author-created documents regarding AI use in nursing practice settings, and (2) improve the readability of the text. After using this service, the author further reviewed and edited the content as needed and takes full responsibility for the content of the chapter.

CHAPTER 13

Conclusions

Decreasing reimbursement will likely be the norm for the foreseeable future. Therefore, financial prudence and management are the responsibility of everyone who works in a healthcare setting—including nurse managers. Indeed, nurse managers are crucial to managing an organization's resources. Nursing budgets generally comprise about 50% of an organization's overall budget. Because nursing is the largest department in most healthcare organizations, nurses have a unique ability to control costs. Human capital is by far the greatest expense in a nursing budget. Controlling labor costs while still balancing quality, safety, and workforce sustainability is one of the most fiscally prudent things a nurse manager can do. This can be achieved by:

- Staffing to meet the budgeted nursing hours per patient day
- Minimizing overtime expenditures or premium labor dependence
- Questioning whether a unit really needs additional personnel
- Changing the skill mix of staff to more sustainably fulfill staffing needs

- Involving staff in meaningful discussions related to staffing and budgets
- Staying abreast of trends
- Utilizing acuity measures to help predict staffing needs

To accomplish this, nurse managers must review current work processes. For example, as a nurse manager, you might explore whether the change-of-shift report could be shortened so it does not involve overtime hours (and by extension, overtime dollars). Are there computerized tools for handoff that still ensure a safe, warm handoff for patients? Do we consider the essential elements of the report off? Are new best practices being utilized or piloted? Overtime reduction often comes from end-to-end workflow design (admissions/discharges, documentation burden, coverage plans, throughput). You might also consider whether supplies could be managed more judiciously. Often, involving staff in these discussions is very helpful. We all know how we take in extra supplies to our rooms "just in case." Explore the cost of doing so with the unit staff, and I guarantee that they will come up with very creative ways to impact the bottom line!

NOTE

People generally think it's no big deal when supplies are overused. But if every department within an organization overuses supplies, it quickly adds up!

These aren't the only things nurse managers should do to improve the finances of their organization, however. Following are five action points to help nurse managers improve the bottom line for their organization and for healthcare in general. Review these and assess how you can apply them at your organization. Then read about how you can better embrace change.

Action Point 1: Get Politically Involved

Many people feel that *politics* is a bad word. Over the years, though, I have learned that we all must use politics to benefit ourselves and our organizations. With respect to politics that relate to reimbursement, nurse managers must align with their organization and with their chief executive officer (CEO) in the effort to secure more funding for the delivery of health services. Nurse managers should understand and follow organizational guidance on advocacy and public policy engagement, and distinguish personal civic engagement from representing the organization, however.

NOTE

Think about it: What would happen to you if your healthcare organization closed? Where would you seek employment? Even if your hospital remains open, it will still need adequate funding for expenses such as salary raises.

Understanding the Role of PACs

Most CEOs belong to the American Hospital Association and their respective state hospital association—for example, the New Jersey Hospital Association or the Hospital Association of Pennsylvania. Large organizations like these, as well as the American Nurses Association, AARP, professional organizations, and others, have political action committees (PACs). PACs take voluntary contributions from members and use the funds to influence legislation and support political candidates aligned with their interests. Donations to PACs are voluntary and not tax-deductible.

The take-home message here is to get politically involved—at the grassroots, state, and federal levels. All these levels have a role in funding healthcare. This means writing, calling, or emailing your local, state, and federal representatives and urging them to support legislation that funds healthcare and helps uninsured individuals obtain insurance. These folks are there to represent us, and we need to make our issues known to them. (It goes without saying that you should also be a registered voter. Otherwise, what is in it for the politicians who seek your vote?) If you want to know where to get started, consider your professional organization. Most of them have local, state, and national committees dedicated to staying abreast of the upcoming bills and legislation on deck. Reach out and participate in what is often known as a Day on the Hill. Take the time to meet with legislators and/or their aides. I found they appreciate real-life examples and value the opinions and experiences of nurses.

NOTE

In addition to engaging in politics on a local, state, and federal level, you must know how to navigate the politics of your organization. All nurses should develop this critical skill.

Action Point 2: Know What Types of Insurance Plans Reimburse Your Organization

Nurse managers must become familiar with the types of insurance products available in the geographic area in which they practice. If you aren't sure what payer mix and payment models are out there, check with someone in your finance department who handles insurance contracts. These individuals can tell you which insurance companies, state programs, and federal programs reimburse your organization. They can even break these numbers down by percentage.

You should also ask your finance department to provide you with a breakdown of the *types* of reimbursements your unit receives. For example, if you are a medical-surgical unit at a healthcare facility that serves a large elderly population, most of your unit's revenue likely comes from Medicare. On the other hand, if you manage an obstetrics nursing unit, the majority of your unit's revenue may come from ACA marketplace plans.

Real-World Example From Al Rundio: Medicare Reimbursements

When I was a chief nursing officer (CNO), Medicare reimbursements accounted for about 55% of our total revenue. Because reimbursements from Medicare tend to be lower than those from other insurers, we had to contract with other insurers that reimbursed at a higher level to make up the difference. Things were even more difficult for another hospital about 90 miles away. Because it served a large retirement community, Medicare reimbursements accounted for 90% of its revenue. This facility had to manage dollars even more judiciously than we did!

Reimbursement money is not a bottomless pit. For example, suppose that during the next fiscal year, Medicare reimbursements at your hospital were reduced by 4%. Suppose further that your hospital's annual reimbursements from Medicare average around $100 million, meaning a 4% reduction would equal $4 million. You might think a $4 million reduction on a $100 million budget is not terribly significant, but suppose your CEO had approved a 4% across-the-board raise. How could your CEO meet that obligation if a major source of reimbursement had been cut by 4%? My point is that to understand and construct budgets, nurse managers must have a grasp of the big picture.

NOTE

Remember: Budgets are based on projected patient volume and the type and amount of reimbursement for those patients.

Action Point 3: Develop Strategic Relationships With Key Individuals in Your Organization

The hospital CFO is a powerful ally. Think about it: As the person who holds the purse strings, the CFO is responsible for making sure the hospital has a positive bottom line. So, nurse managers must establish an excellent relationship with their CFO.

There are other key personnel in their organization's finance department—the ones who know the nuts and bolts of finance—with whom nurse managers should establish good relations. These individuals help create the budgets for the organization. Some of them negotiate managed care contracts; others generate patient bills based on what occurred during the patient's hospital stay. These individuals can help nurse managers gain a better understanding of finance, reimbursement, managed care, and billing.

When I was CNO I was fortunate to have an amazing CFO who always worked with me to help find the funds for projects or to plan a way to get the funds in the near future.

NOTE

As a manager, you must reach out to others in your organization. You must work closely with them to understand where they are coming from. Remember: You want others to serve the nursing department. This only happens when you have positive working relationships based on mutual trust and understanding.

Action Point 4: Speak the Language of Finance

Before delving into the subject of actually speaking the language of finance, let's discuss communication in more general terms. Communication is the lifeblood of any organization. It's critical to the organization's success.

NOTE

Communication can occur in an upward manner (from subordinate to manager), in a downward manner (from manager to subordinate), and in a lateral manner (across the organization).

Understanding Communication Processes

Communication consists of a number of processes on the part of both the "sender" and the "receiver" of the message. Communication processes for the sender are as follows:

1. The sender identifies an idea that they want to communicate, such as an increase in a supply expense.
2. The sender frames the idea in some format that can be communicated (for example, an email message, a letter, a text, a nonverbal message, or a verbal message). The sender considers the appropriate means of communication.
3. The sender sends the message using the selected format—an email with a read receipt.

Communication processes for the receiver include the following:

1. The receiver receives the message.
2. The receiver reviews the message.
3. The receiver perceives and interprets the meaning of the message.

With each process, miscommunication is a risk. So, to ensure effective communication—communication that is comprehensive and accurately understood—you want to remain mindful of these processes from the perspective of both the sender and the receiver. It is especially important to understand the components of communication when sharing information about financial performance with staff and administration.

The Benefits of Face-to-Face Communication

These days, a lot of communication occurs through email. While email can be great—especially for sharing financial reports, so people can review them at their own pace—it omits the nonverbal cues that are visible when speaking with someone face to face. (Note that face-to-face communication does not necessarily require the individuals communicating to be in the same room. Much face-to-face communication now occurs through telecommunication platforms like Zoom, FaceTime, and Teams.)

Getting the Lingo Down

Different departments in different organizations speak different languages. Take nursing as an example—the abbreviations we use, and even the slang. A lot of people have no clue what we are talking about. The same is true of members of the finance department.

If you want to bond with members of the finance department, you must learn to speak their language. I have often found that our finance department enjoys partnering with nursing leaders to help set the stage for the basic finance definitions and available reports. When they understand the exact needs of the nurse leaders, they are often able to revise reports to make them more meaningful for the leader and ultimately make an impact on the organization.

My advice is to memorize and understand key financial terms. (Refer to the section "A Glossary of Basic Accounting Terms" in Chapter 3.) Then, use these terms on a regular basis with administrators and finance personnel. By being able to talk the talk, nurse managers will gain not only the respect of the finance department but also the clout to get needed resources for their department.

Real-Work Example From Al Rundio: Financial Education

Early in my career, one of my biggest concerns was my weakness in finance. I'd taken financial management courses in college, and I knew how to manage a budget. But I wasn't familiar with key financial terms like *amortization, zero-based budgeting,* and so on. Fortunately, when I was getting my master's degree in nursing, a professor suggested I memorize and master these terms. This sage advice has taken me far!

Action Point 5: Practice Finance

Just as a pianist masters the craft by continuously practicing the piano, to really grasp the meaning of finance, you must practice it. That means doing the following:

- Getting comfortable with reviewing financial reports
- Working with finance to obtain reports that you can easily interpret
- Taking an active—rather than passive—role in the preparation of the budget
- Questioning things in the process of creating the budget with finance

Most importantly, you should monitor budget performance by comparing actual expenses with budgeted ones. For example, if the aggregate numbers look good, overall expenses are under budget, and patient volume is down, but overtime increases for the RN staff, ask why. If it turns out the overtime was unnecessary, correct it, and make sure it does not happen in the next period. The key is to take corrective action when warranted based on the financial reports and statistics.

Putting Financial Principles in Action

A CNO wanted his nurse managers to gain a better understanding of financial reports so they could better control expenses, especially those related to overtime. The hospital's payroll and associated financial reports ran every other Tuesday. So, for about six months, the CNO, the finance department budget manager, and the nurse managers met every other Wednesday to discuss them. During these meetings, the nurse managers learned how to read and interpret these reports. They then applied the principles they learned and significantly reduced overtime in the process.

Embracing Change

Nurse managers must manage fiscally sound units. Although providing quality care is paramount, controlling expenses is also critical. Achieving both of these aims often means embracing change. For example, you might need to implement a new staffing model that improves quality and controls costs. One such model might incorporate patient care techs so that the patient's basic needs are met in a timelier manner. Or you might need to introduce new tools from an upgrade to the electronic health records system to document care more quickly, easily, and accurately.

Embracing change means adopting the change process. Social scientist Kurt Lewin describes three steps of the change process as follows (Huber, 2013).

Step 1: Unfreezing

In this stage, you do the following:

1. Gather data.
2. Diagnose the problem.

3. Decide whether a change is needed to solve the problem.
4. Make others aware of the need for change.

NOTE

The motivation for change should begin in this stage.

Step 2: Movement

Step 2 is the movement phase. This is where you:

1. Develop a formal plan.
2. Formulate goals and objectives.
3. Identify areas of support and resistance.

NOTE

It is important to include everyone who will be affected by the change in the planning process. People are more apt to buy into change when they are part of the change process.

Nursing staff must be involved in this phase to gain a sense of fiscal awareness and to ensure they know the goals and objectives of the unit. They must also be aware of what types of reports will be generated and what action will be taken if, for example, a variance exists.

This is also the stage when strategies are developed for implementing the change. It is important that nurse managers are available to support others through the change process and to offer encouragement as needed.

During this step, nurse managers must consider how to overcome resistance to the change. For example, they may need to explain why overtime must be used judiciously. They might also need to explain that the need for overtime must be demonstrated before they assign overtime hours.

Step 3: Refreezing

In this stage, the change becomes a permanent part of the organization. This is also the stage in which the change is evaluated. If a review of financial reports reveals a problem with the change, the nurse manager and staff must be open to adjustments. A common adjustment is to staffing levels. For example, the unit might need to employ additional RNs to provide a higher RN-to-patient ratio. Or the unit might need to assess the competencies of staff to better care for higher-acuity patients. What's critical is for the staff and the nurse manager to plan strategies for adjustments and to remain open to revisions when necessary so that optimal patient care can be provided in a cost-effective environment.

NOTE

Nurse managers must remain available during this phase to support others so that the change remains in place.

In Closing

Updating Al Rundio's book for this fourth edition was like editing a sacred text. I kept some of Al's examples and added a few others to help bring the budgeting process to life. I hope this book has provided you with the tools to embrace the financial aspects of your organization and of your own unit(s), as well as the budget process—most importantly, monitoring and managing the budget.

As mentioned, early in my career, finance was not a strong suit. But after learning the budget process in depth, I found finance and budgeting to be the most enjoyable part of my job. It was challenging but rewarding to see positive results when I managed the budget and finances correctly. I enjoyed negotiating to get the best possible resources for our staff and ultimately our patients.

Of course, learning is a continuous process. I was reminded of this over and over when the COVID-19 pandemic struck in 2020. Navigating this pandemic—which will most likely *not* be the last one we experience—has certainly shed new light on finance and budgets in healthcare settings. We have learned much about how to maintain supply levels and to manage finances, emergency preparedness, and staff in such situations.

Al loved swimming, and so do I. So, I think I can speak for him when I say we encourage you to take the plunge! Dive into the waters of finance. You may start with the basic doggy paddle, but soon you will be able to swim with the sharks and frolic with the dolphins (they are my favorite!).

Summary

This chapter discussed the following:

- Getting politically involved
- Knowing what types of insurance plans reimburse your organization
- Developing strategic relationships with key individuals in your organization
- Speaking the language of finance
- Practicing finance
- Embracing change

"Budgeting is not about limiting yourself; it is about making the things that excite you happen!"

–Unknown

Reference

Huber, D. L. (2013). *Leadership & nursing care management* (5th ed.). Elsevier.

Index

Note: Page references noted with an *f* are figures; page references noted with a *t* are tables.

C

D

G

H

I

www.ingramcontent.com/pod-product-compliance
Ingram Content Group UK Ltd.
Pitfield, Milton Keynes, MK11 3LW, UK
UKHW051447290926
15471UKWH00008B/1068

9 781646 482221